STOP

HOMOCYSTEINE
Through the
METHYLATION
PROCESS

D0684350

Stop Homocysteine Through The Methylation Process is not intended as medical advice. Its intention is solely informational and educational. Please consult a health care professional if clinically indicated.

Stop Homocysteine Through The Methylation Process.
Paul Frankel, Ph.D., Fred Madsen, Ph.D.
  With James Lembeck, D.Ch., C.H.,
        and preface by Julian Whitaker, M.D.

First Edition - April, 1998, revised May, 1998

Printed in the United States of America

Published by:
The Research Corner, Publications
1336 Moorpark Road, #168
Thousand Oaks, CA 91360
(805) 449-5252

To the memories of those whose absence is a continual reminder of the fleeting and precious qualities of life.

ABOUT THE AUTHORS

Paul Frankel, Ph.D. received his degree in Applied Mathematics specializing in Mathematical Biology from Brown University in Providence, RI in 1992. He was a Juvenile Diabetes Fellow and the first predoctoral IRTA Fellow at the National Institutes of Health. He was a Visiting Assistant Professor of Mathematics at the University of Southern California and a volunteer at the City of Hope studying cell culture techniques. In 1995, Dr. Frankel founded The Research Corner; a company devoted to medical research, updates and educational services. He has published articles in peer-reviewed medical and research journals, in addition to the popular press. In 1996 he published a booklet entitled Beyond AntiOxidants: Methylation, Homocysteine and Nutrition, followed by the 1997 booklet Your Life Depends On It! Methylation, Homocysteine and Your Health with Dr. Madsen. These booklets resulted not from his academic interest in the topic, but stemmed from experience using the technology for his own health crisis. Dr. Frankel is one of the strongest supporters of dietary methyl donors, especially TMG (trimethylglycine). Dr. Frankel continues to do research in this field as well as helping both companies and scientists conduct research projects related to human health.

While it may seem incongruous, Dr. Frankel is both health conscious and a rock-climber. In the morning in Las Vegas you may see him give a lecture on the health risks of eating poorly, and in the afternoon you may see him on Red Rocks, hundreds of feet above the ground. The fact that he is exceedingly careful about his diet indicates which he considers the greater risk to long term health (he does use a safety rope!).

Dr. Fred Madsen earned a Ph.D. in Animal Nutrition-Physiology from the University of Tennessee in Knoxville in 1974. He spent two years at the Comparative Animal Research Laboratory in Oak Ridge, Tennessee before working for the pharmaceutical company, Syntex. In 1979 he returned to Knoxville and worked in the animal feed business. During the following 18 years in the feed industry, he learned the art of animal nutrition. He is a member of several scientific organizations, including the American Society for Nutritional Sciences (formally the American Institute of Nutrition), and has lectured worldwide on a variety of topics related to disease and diet. Dr. Madsen has written numerous articles in scientific and popular journals. After losing stomach acidity during a trip to China in 1986, he successfully used betaine-HCL to regain his health. Dr. Madsen then investigated betaine without the HCL, and gained a new appreciation for methylation, becoming aware of its role in the battle against aging and degenerative diseases. Many people are now recognizing that animals are fed better than most humans, and only a handful of animal nutritionists lead the way in the use of diet in the prevention of disease. Dr. Madsen is one of the best in his field.

Dr. Jim Lembeck received a doctoral degree in holistic preventive medicine from Lafayette University, and a certification in herbal medicine from Westbrook University. He specializes in sports nutrition and writes a monthly column in *Men's Exercise Magazine* and the *Great Lakes Fitness Guide*. He is in the Who's Who in the West and the Who's Who in America, and has personal experience with methyl donors in performance. Dr. Lembeck has been a consultant to the nutrition industry for almost two decades.

PREFACE

The benefits of antioxidants in reducing the risk of cardiovascular disease, cancer, and other degenerative diseases are by now familiar to most of us. A less well known but equally important group of protective compounds are the methyl donors. Methyl donors — folate, vitamin B-12 and trimethylglycine (TMG) — play a vital role in preventing the principal cause of cardiovascular disease: elevated homocysteine levels.

It is a sad commentary on the medical establishment that this knowledge was available to us as early as 1969 — more than 25 years ago. That's when Harvard pathologist Kilmer S. McCully proposed that elevated homocysteine — not high cholesterol — was the primary causative factor in atherosclerosis. Dr. McCully observed that children with a genetic deficiency that resulted in high homocysteine levels had heart disease and severe artery damage similar to that seen in much older persons. Subsequent research has borne out this hypothesis, although news has been slow to get to the general public.

Drs. Frankel and Madsen have provided a great service by clearly elaborating in this book the importance of methyl donors and methylation in reducing homocysteine levels and preventing heart disease. As you'll see in the following pages methylation also plays a crucial role in protecting our DNA. Loss of methyl groups occurs as cells degenerate, resulting in inappropriate gene expression, which has implications for some cancers as well as the general aging process.

I've been advocating the fundamentals of diet, lifestyle, and supplementation for over 25 years. And over time, research has repeatedly borne out the importance of all three of these factors in maintaining health and preventing disease. Drs. Frankel and Madsen elucidate yet another degenerative pathway that can be averted by the combination of a nutritious diet, a healthy lifestyle, and judicious supplementation.

— Julian Whitaker, M.D.

AUTHORS' NOTES

From the Desk of Paul Frankel, Ph.D.

While a good doctor is always helpful, one's own vigilance is critical. It saved me from heart surgery in 1981, a back surgery in 1985, and abdominal surgery in 1995. The technology presented in this book played a significant role in avoiding the last one.

Such life experiences, combined with a rigorous research oriented training, change a person. The focus becomes clear, and any preconceived ideas or blind faith becomes as harmful to health research as the involvement of notions such as ego or pride.

As part of this ongoing research, I found myself in the mountains of southern California on a research retreat with scientists from The City of Hope, in Duarte, California. Invited by Dr. Robert Klevecz, a cell biologist famous for his work in drug timing effects, I was watching the usual parade of world-class researchers present their latest material. Up stepped a youthful, quiet, researcher, Dr. Craig Cooney. Given his suit, and spectacles, he looked 30. In a T-shirt and on roller blades he could have passed for a college student.

It was 1993, and Dr. Cooney was presenting work on methylation and aging that he had been working on since 1979. The topic was completely foreign to me, but the presentation was clear, and somehow I sensed the material was different and exciting. I made a point of sitting next to Craig at dinner. During the course of the meal, and remembering that his work focused on aging, I joked:

"Well, if you are 20 years old, your theory won't go very far."

I had no idea that he was nearly 40! Fortunately, given the tone, we all laughed. I don't even remember if he answered. Even to this day, every time I remember his age, I am amazed. For nearly a year after Craig's talk, I followed methylation research, while pursuing my own interests in feedback and coupling in cancer. After discovering that these two research paths were intertwined, I became an avid student of methylation metabolism.

At that time, Craig's research, and mine, would have remained shelved under "academic" had I not faced a real and personal problem that forced me to seek practical ways of trying to help my liver. I tried this new methylation technology (combined with Chinese herbs and a cleansing program), and was amazed with the results... so were my physicians.

Sadly, however, only a handful of people were aware of the role of methylation in human health. Two years later I had produced a short booklet summarizing some of the most important research, and now, almost four years later, I have teamed up with one of the leaders in animal nutrition, Fred Madsen, to produce this book. Interestingly, Fred had used methylation in his animal nutrition business, having independently realized the power of methylation and diet. Combining his years of experience using methylation in practical animal nutrition with the human research on homocysteine, TMG, and more, we have been able to synthesize the relevant science in a way that has demonstrated its ability to improve the human condition.

Paul Frankel, Ph.D., 1998

My interest in methylation started over 25 years ago in graduate school at the University of Tennessee. While in graduate school, I was fortunate to have studied methylation metabolism (It later became critical for planning optimal diets for commercial farms). The role of methylation in converting homocysteine to methionine was being taught along with many of the biochemical reactions that use methylation. We were studying the results of research in animals and humans that showed that defects in the way we detoxify homocysteine lead to a variety of diseases. However, no one at the time, except maybe Dr. McCully, had made the connection between "normal" levels of plasma homocysteine and heart disease in the general population, not to mention the other diseases and aging associated with poor methylation. Initially, my own interests in homocysteine and methylation didn't extend beyond passing exams.

Methylation became more than an academic subject once I started to work and study in the area of animal nutrition. I learned as most animal nutritionists have, particularly poultry nutritionists, that the methyl donors methionine and choline are important components of the diet. It was, and still is, standard practice to carefully balance these nutrients for optimal health and growth in a wide variety of animal species.

What intrigued me most however, was what other areas of animal performance could be manipulated through controlling methylation. There are over 100 separate reactions in the body that use methyl groups. It was clear that the potential was tremendous for improved animal performance through methyl group manipulation.

The first methylation system I exploited in animal nutrition was the liver detoxifying pathways, which used methyl groups to safely remove toxic plant pigments from the body.

Plant breeders were producing varieties of grain designed to stop wild birds from eating the crop. They did this by enhancing the level of toxic compounds naturally present in the grain. However, animal nutritionists and livestock producers had to feed this grain to animals and poultry, which are very similar metabolically to the wild birds which didn't want to eat the grain in the first place. Part of the answer was to increase the methyl donor supply in the diet so that the toxic materials could be more effectively detoxified and excreted from the animal.

After this, other exciting opportunities arose to use or manipulate methyl group metabolism to enhance animal performance and reduce the risk of disease. I found that control of methyl group metabolism was instrumental in keeping animals calm in captivity or during high stress situations. Also, I discovered that lean body mass could be increased in poultry with methylation techniques. It seems strange now, but at the time I never even considered using the technology for myself.

It was during 1986 that I became ill after a consulting trip to China and for reasons other than methylation, I started using betaine HCl in hopes that it would help me get over the digestive problems I was experiencing. It worked, and I have continued taking betaine HCl for nearly 12 years. It wasn't until the last 3 years, however, that I realized, through the publications of Dr. Frankel and the recent clinical data, how important the methylation part of betaine HCl is to reducing the risk of heart disease and other diseases of aging.

11

As a result, my interests in methylation heightened again and I started to investigate the possibility that methylation could influence viral disease in animals.

As I look back on my years since college, I seem to have been led down a path to a better understanding of metabolism and disease in farm animals, which has resulted in a more thorough understanding of the needs of my own body. I really never thought that this journey would result in a book that would help other people improve their lives.

Fred Madsen, Ph.D., 1998.

ACKNOWLEDGEMENTS

The authors wish to acknowledge the generous and invaluable assistance by giving a special thank you to: Dr. Kilmer McCully, for his support and advice, and for his ground breaking research in 1969 which launched this new era of homocysteine and methylation; Dr. Craig Cooney, for his leading work in methylation, his friendship, and his unswerving dedication; Dr. Herminio Reyes whose efforts and influences are unmistakable in the very format of the book; Alex, Carrie, Terri and Janet, who were helpful in various stages of the development of the writing and presentation; Dino, Raymond, and Richard, and Ron for their artwork contributions, and most importantly to our friends and families, whose quiet and patient support allowed us the strength to finish this book.

TABLE OF CONTENTS

I

PROLOGUE TO THE SEARCH

"seek, and ye shall find" – Matthew 8:7

Juan Ponce De León, a Spanish conqueror who traveled with Christopher Columbus on the second voyage, is most famous for his search for the fountain of youth. Like Columbus, Ponce De León thought he was in the Far East, when in fact he had just conquered Puerto Rico.

Following an Indian legend regarding a fountain that restores youth, he went on a search for the island of Bimini. In 1509 he landed and explored a land mass he called Florida ("full of flowers"). Drinking from every spring he came upon, he never found the elusive fountain of youth. He died 8 years later trying to colonize Florida.

Nearly 500 years later, we have continued the search to improve the quality of life, not in a stream, or fountain, but through the amazing world of science.

The results of our search are anything but ordinary. The techniques have been PROVEN to:

➤ **Reduce the level of certain dangerous chemicals that rise with age.**

➤ **Reduce some of the changes that occur in the cells as animals age.**

➢ Reduce the incidence of age-related diseases including heart disease and cancer.

➢ Reduce the level of chemicals that are associated with faster death in individuals who already have heart disease.

➢ Improve the functioning of the liver and promote neurological health, two conditions that get more common and serious with age.

➢ Improve antioxidant protection.

➢ Extend the life of a large number of people.

We age cell by cell, day by day. Slowing the deterioration of the cells, improving the integrity of our tissues, and efficiently removing toxic chemicals from the body will extend the quality of your life.

II

INTRODUCTION (CONNECTIONS)

The last time I saw my great grandmother Anna alive, we had a wonderful time. I ate her special rugelach cookies and laughed at the tales of her younger days. She entertained us with the story of one of her husbands, after whom I was named. He was a traveling tailor, walking the streets of New York with a sewing machine on his back. He was a lousy tailor, and hence he had to keep moving since he rarely had a repeat customer.

The next time I saw her was at her funeral. I didn't even know she'd been sick. Why didn't anyone tell me? I later discovered that it was an unspoken rule to not talk about such things. I finally realized that health talk follows a rather consistent pattern:

First Person: How are you?

Second Person: Fine, thank you. How have you been?

First Person: Good. (or if deathly ill, "Good, considering").

Whether it is with friends or relatives, people deceive one another about health. At the funeral I wondered how she was really doing before she died. I asked my parents. Apparently, she was a prisoner in her own apartment for nearly five years prior to the funeral. For the past 10 years she had extreme leg pains and could barely navigate the stairs. BUT … she was always cheerful and had pleasant things to say…

The net result is that even though nearly 100 million people suffer from premature loss of quality of life in the U.S., each keeps it secret, sometimes even from their closest friends and family. The remaining 200 million think it will never happen to them because it seems to be a rare part of their family life.

Even hospitals are set up to maintain the self-denial. Visiting hours are short, so patients can muster up the strength to look good for a short period of time to people on the outside. I remember my uncle was getting ready for his young son to visit him in the hospital. He wanted to look as healthy as possible. Laying in bed, he said: "Sorry, I am trying to look my best for when my son comes in, so I'm going to have to nap now". "Sorry?" The poor man was dying, he knew it, and was "Sorry" he couldn't put on a show for us, as he was saving it up for his son. He was violating the unwritten law to pretend that everything is okay. Everything is not okay.

In 1994 there were 22,279,000 Americans suffering from heart disease, 33,446,000 suffering from arthritis, 7,766,000 fighting the effects of diabetes, and 28,236,000 trying to survive high blood pressure.

Between 10 and 15 percent of the U.S. population had to limit their activity during 1994, and older folks lost an average of one month per year through challenges to their health. More than 5 million people need daily assistance for activities such as bathing, dressing, preparing meals, and even using the telephone. One and a half million people are in nursing homes, and in 1995, there were more than 800,000 operations on the heart alone (by-pass surgery, angioplasty etc.).

In addition, in 1996, 733,834 people died of heart disease, another 160,431 from cerebrovascular disease, 544,278 from cancer, 61,559 from diabetes, 32,655 from AIDS, and 25,135 from liver disease.

The number of people dying and suffering from degenerative diseases is beyond comprehension, if not absolutely numbing. When statistics were presented on people killed in concentration camps or battles in World War II, no one could comprehend the human suffering, and people tuned it out or went into a strange form of denial. The same was true of the Civil War, World War I, and nearly every war previous to the Vietnam War. Finally, in Vietnam, television opened the country's eyes to the suffering caused by armed conflict. Compared to previous modern U.S. wars, far fewer people were killed, but the personalization through the media finally put war in perspective.

The same process of disinterest in numbers keeps people from facing the reality of human suffering here at home, stopping people from facing the reality that blind faith in allopathic medicine is unwarranted. We can do much better.

By using proper diet, lifestyle and supplements, between 50% and 75% of the suffering and loss of quality of life due to heart and vascular disease can be prevented. This will result in more years of love, happiness, and fulfillment. This is not hype, but peer-reviewed, scientific fact. Similarly, human suffering due to other degenerative diseases can also be reduced.

It is never too late to alter your diet and lifestyle, and the sooner the better.

What led us to the material in the book was a simple approach. We noticed that many of the natural diets or nutritional therapies had a lot in common. We also noticed that they were proposed as a treatment for many degenerative diseases – from heart disease, to cancer, arthritis and even AIDS. In addition, through personal experience, we noted that sometimes these therapies worked. We knew then of the awesome power of nutrition in humans (although we were already aware of its near total effect on the health of animals). We investigated what these natural healing diets have in common, and looked for a common thread. We figured that if the same therapy addresses so many diseases, then the diseases would have commonality. By pursuing these commonalities, a deeper understanding into the workings of the human healing potential was obtained. We then took advantage of this through a focused program of dietary modifications and supplements to maintain proper health, seeking peer-reviewed scientific verification of our concept.

We found a common thread, and succeeded in developing a plan to enhance the body's health and extend the quality of life. We were pleased that it linked up with some of the most promising anti-aging theories. The program was developed to help normal people prevent obvious unraveling of this common thread. It is solidly backed by clinical trials and scientific studies.

We still need to work harder. The truth of healing is still unknown. The difference between preventing disease through adequate nutrition, and healing disease through a combination of targeted nutrition and other healing modalities is enormous.

This latter step will take years to develop, and requires intense research. To state anything else would defeat the purpose of trying to encourage others to take the torch and maximize the benefits obtainable through dietary manipulation of the strongest link to health known today, **METHYLATION**.

As you read this book, consider who wrote it. Unlike Kipling, Shakespeare, or even Tom Clancy, we are neither fiction writers nor "science writers", but scientists. As a result, the following text is dense with facts. Unlike most health books, it is fully referenced, so you, the reader, can verify and investigate any point that interests you. We could not imagine doing anything less. To make it easier to read, we have concluded each section with a *take home message*. In addition, we tried to lighten things up with a few cartoons. But make no mistake, this is an information book, not a pleasure reading novel.

We believe, but are not sure, that Methuselah, an older gentleman living in the middle east, may have been the first to discover the benefits of methylation.

III

BREAKTHROUGHS IN HEALTH
(CLUES AND TEASERS)

*"Don't put in Jim's medical testimony – nobody would
believe it!" –* Editor

Testing the water from every well and spring was Ponce De
León's method of trial. We are using science. It does not mean
that we only pay attention to peer-reviewed double-blind
placebo controlled trials. Such trials are like the bread crumbs
left by Hansel and Gretel. They mark the progress of other
explorers. In our search, we naturally must know where others
have gone. However, it is by straying off the path and watching
carefully for clues and hints that really helps us know what
direction to take next. Such clues are often the response of a
friend or ourselves to a new dietary plan. These clues, called
anecdotal reports, are used to gain insight into where we look
for peer-reviewed verification, and how we plan future
research.

Aside from our own personal experiences, our first clues came
from "unscientific" attempts to turn our friends and family into
methylation guinea pigs. While heart disease is often silent and
goes unnoticed, our test cases were not. We soon found out that
methylation worked.

*Mike, a 45-year old plumber, had severe genital herpes. He
suffered from nearly 12 eruptions a year, each one agonizingly
painful. Over a period of 10 years he tried everything to
decrease the severity of this disease, and nothing helped. Then
he started taking large doses of TMG (trimethylglycine —*

that's "tri" as in 3, methyl as in CH3, and glycine as in the amino acid). His eruptions disappeared for nearly six months, and only recurred after he ran himself down by not sleeping for three nights.

A 16-year old Japanese girl couldn't walk, and had muscle weakness and pain in her arms and legs. It was discovered that she had a genetic disorder that reduced her body's ability to form SAM, a methyl donor. After two months of adding TMG to her list of dietary supplements, there was a marked improvement and she was able to walk with support. After 17 months of therapy with dietary methyl donors she was free from her gait disturbance and muscle weakness and was able to decrease her medications [a peer-reviewed case study (see T. Kishi, et al)].

Dorothy, a grandmother with adult diabetes, has been taking the methyl donor supplements suggested in this book for several months. Her glycated hemoglobin, a measure of the total amount of blood glucose she was exposed to over a period of several months, dropped from 8.4 to 7.9 since taking the supplement. Normal is 4.0-6.9.

Pete, a 46-year old executive in the feed supplement industry, has been taking the methyl donor supplements for two months. Pete has a history of cardiovascular disease (heart attack and balloon angioplasty). Pete's triglycerides were 180 and the methyl donor package brought it down to below 90. In addition, he saw an increase in his HDL and a decrease in his LDL. He also noticed that he does not get stressed out as much. While Pete finds it hard to describe, he says he feels more "even" throughout the day, and seems to have improved digestion.

Bill, a business manager in the animal nutrition business, has been using methyl donors for one month. Bill noticed improved digestion, with more consistent bowel movements.

John, a college student who lifts weights, was using creatine and a rice bran extract. Now that he has added the methyl donor supplements, he has finally had a breakthrough, gaining more muscle mass in a shorter period of time than ever before.

Mary, a 50-year old who suffered from fatigue, started a complete methyl supplement plan as outlined in this book. She immediately regained energy and was able to start working full-time within one month.

Reverend Green, a 45-year old late onset diabetic, started taking the methyl supplement. His eyesight became less blurry, and his blood sugar dropped from 180 to 140 (70-115 is normal). He continues to take both his diabetic medication and the methyl supplement program.

David, generally healthy, noticed a decrease in the frequency and the severity of colds after taking methyl supplements.

These stories and more document only some of the benefits people have been experiencing using the techniques to be discussed, i.e. methylation enhancement and supplementation. What is methyl supplementation, and what are methyl donors? How do they work and how could they provide the miraculous health results that are described above? The following report provides the answers to these questions. *

---

* The case histories presented are not meant to imply that such results are either typical nor guaranteed. Each person reacts differently, and such anecdotal reports do not imply any claim regarding the benefits of the material enclosed. For privacy reasons, all names and identifying data have been changed.

IV

GLOSSARY OF NEW TERMS
(THE LANGUAGE OF THE SEARCH)

Whenever a new topic is introduced, a new vocabulary is required. This is unavoidable. We have, however, gathered some of the key new words (some which are probably not even in your dictionary), and assembled them for you to refer back to as needed.

ATP: adenosine triphosphate, a chemical storehouse for energy used extensively by our body.

Cystathionine β-synthase activity: The enzyme that converts homocysteine to the non-toxic amino acid cystathionine. This enzyme needs vitamin B-6 and SAM (see below) to work properly.

Genetic deficiencies: When people are born with low natural ability to function in a healthy manner, they are said to have a genetic deficiency. In the context of this book it relates to the lowered activity of the enzymes which reduce the toxic amino acid, homocysteine.

DNA: Deoxyribonucleic acid, our genetic blueprint. The DNA encodes for eye color, hair color, enzyme activity, etc., and is the starting point for the building of each and every cell in our body.

Demethylation: Removal of a methyl group from DNA or other biomolecules.

Enzyme: A protein which speeds up the reaction between two or more chemicals.

Homocysteine: A toxic amino acid shown to be a significant risk factor for cardiovascular disease, neural tube defects and more. The abbreviation for homocysteine is HCY.

Homocysteine load: The total amount of homocysteine the body is exposed to in a 24-hour period (i.e. the total toxic exposure).

Homocysteine thiolactone: An altered form of homocysteine. It is more reactive (damaging) towards cell structures and molecules than homocysteine.

Homocysteinemia: The medical term for extremely high levels of homocysteine in blood.

Homocystinuria: excess homocysteine in the urine.

Homocystinuric osteoporosis: Bone loss and weakness found in patients with homocystinuria.

Methionine: A non-toxic amino acid that is found in most proteins and in the natural anti-depressant and methylating agent known as SAM (see below).

Methyl Group: One carbon and three hydrogens. This group attaches to sections of the genetic code and when coupled with homocysteine converts homocysteine to methionine.

Methylation: The process of putting a methyl group onto DNA, homocysteine or other compounds.

Oxidation: To function, your body is burning fuel – mostly carbohydrates and fats – at a low temperature (98.7F). Some of that "fire" damages the cells in our body. That is referred to as oxidative damage.

Oxidative hits: Certain molecules absorb the damage from the burning (see above) to protect a more critical part of your body. These are sacrificed to protect the health of the individual. The manufacture of some of these sacrificial chemicals (antioxidants) requires methylation.

SAM or SAMe: S-adenosylmethionine. A natural anti-depressant and supplier of methyl groups to DNA (DNA methylation) and other molecules in the body.

Trimethylglycine (TMG): A chemical compound and the best known dietary source of methyl groups. TMG is found in a large number of plants and animals, especially broccoli and beets.

Transsulfuration: The process of moving sulfur from the toxic amino acid homocysteine to the non-toxic sulfur amino acids cystathionine, cysteine and taurine.

V

QUOTES FROM THE MEDICAL LITERATURE
(SOME CLUES FROM EARLIER EXPLORERS)

Many health books are poorly referenced, or are written authoritatively, but by the end of the book you realize they are simply spouting opinion. The topic of this book deserves better, and we present this section to provide the reader with quotes from clinical research which establish that we are talking about the most highly referenced and powerful nutritional approach to date.

JAMA[1] (vol. 277, No. 22, pg. 1776-1781, 1997)

"In this study, users of vitamin preparations containing these nutrients appear to experience substantial protection from vascular disease, with a relative risk of 0.38 (95% CI 0.2-0.72) compared with nonusers of vitamins."

[Interpretation: If a group of nonusers of vitamins contained 100 people with diseases of the blood vessels, the same size group of vitamin users would expect only 38 people with vascular disease. This sounds technical, but imagine what it means for a typical family. It means that by properly using vitamins, parents could double their chances of seeing their grandchildren and great grandchildren. It doubles the odds of being a lively senior, playing golf and tennis in your leisure, and taking a simple set of stairs for granted.]

<u>Alternative Medicine Review</u>[2] (vol. 2, No. 4, pg. 234, 1997)

"... numerous diseases of the nervous system are correlated with high homocysteine levels and alterations in B12, folate or B6 metabolism, including depression, schizophrenia, multiple sclerosis, Parkinson's disease, Alzheimer's disease, and cognitive decline in the elderly."

[Interpretation: A variety of age-related mental diseases are related to high levels of homocysteine. These disorders include depression, Parkinson's disease, Alzheimer's disease and a general loss of mental abilities observed in the elderly. Properly correcting these problems through nutrition and supplementation goes a long way in reversing or preventing this "unnatural" decline observed all too often in our western "unnatural" culture.]

<u>JAMA</u>[3] (vol. 268, pg. 877-881. Aug 12, 1992)

"Moderately high levels of plasma homocyst(e)ine are associated with subsequent risk of MI (myocardial infarction) independent of other coronary risk factors. Because high levels can often be easily treated with vitamin supplements, homocyst(e)ine may be an independent, modifiable, risk factor."

[Interpretation: The higher the level of homocysteine the higher the probability of a heart attack. In addition, this level can be safely reduced with simple dietary supplements.]

VI

THE STORY OF METHYLATION
(WHERE WE ARE GOING)

Since you are reading this book, you probably share the goal of living a long and healthy life. Unexpectedly, four simple dietary supplements have unprecedented power to help: folic acid, vitamin B-12, vitamin B-6 and trimethylglycine (TMG). None of them are antioxidants, but they probably have a larger effect on the overall antioxidant defense than compounds normally classified as dietary antioxidants. That is only the tip of the iceberg.

Folic acid, B-12, B-6 and TMG are part of methylation, a chemical process in the body working against cancer, heart disease, neurological disease, liver disease, and nearly every age-related disorder. In addition, these nutrients are part of a program developed by Dr. Craig Cooney to retard aging.

Methylation is not easy to explain. Basically a chemistry concept, it is full of words and ideas that are largely unfamiliar to both scientists and the health conscious population. Therefore, we provided a glossary in the beginning of the book, and have attempted to ease the reader into the topic. We hope, like Ravel's "Bolero", that towards the end, the excitement reaches such a peak that you can no longer contain yourself – as we obviously could not.

VII

METHYLATION: A KEY MECHANISM TO UNDERSTANDING HEALTH AND AGING (THE FIRST REVELATION)

"until at last it came to me that time was suspect" – Albert Einstein

Recent research indicates that the process known as methylation is directly related to many diseases, including cancer, heart disease, liver disease, and neurological disorders. Furthermore, methylation also appears to play a significant role in the aging process in general. Methylation can be enhanced or inhibited through diet, lifestyle factors (such as smoking, drinking and taking birth control pills – all of which decrease methylation), and direct supplementation, primarily with folic acid, B-12 and TMG.

"Trimethylglycine," "methylation," and other terms yet to come, are relatively new or obscure. Soon, these new terms will become as commonplace and familiar as "antioxidants," "beta-carotene," and "free radicals." For now, the new words may seem daunting, but by the time you have finished this book, the words will not seem so foreign. In fact, the term "methylation" may become a friend as it has to us and others.

What It Is

Methylation is the process by which methyl groups (CH_3 – a molecule consisting of one carbon atom and three hydrogen atoms) attach to different substances in the body, working to either protect or transform them. For instance, when properly attached to DNA, methyl groups can act in a protective capacity, keeping inappropriate genes (i.e. genes that manifest as disease or disorder) from being expressed.[4]

Methyl groups (in the presence of appropriate enzymes) are best known for their role in converting homocysteine, a toxic amino acid, to methionine, an essential amino acid, required for the production of proteins and natural antidepressants. Methylation is also well known for its effect on fat metabolism and liver detoxification.

Aging and Methylation

Methylation is a naturally occurring process; Methylation decreases as we age. As we get older, methyl groups are lost from DNA, and the ability to replace methyl groups (or methylate) is decreased.[4] Optimal methylation (as indicated by low homocysteine) is usually found in young women of childbearing years†.

Methylation can be affected by many different external factors that work to either inhibit or enhance the ability to methylate. Some of the factors that can cause methyl deficiencies, in addition to aging are:

1. High fat diet
2. Cigarette smoking
3. Birth control pills
4. Diets low in vegetables and whole grains
5. Genetic predisposition
6. Belonging to the male gender

---

† Note that methylation and homocysteine levels while related, are not the same.

Factors that can be used to <u>enhance</u> methylation are: diets high in methyl groups such as TMG, and nutrients used in the processing of methyl groups such as folic acid (with vitamin B-12), and to a lesser extent choline, choline containing lipids, and methionine‡.

Take Home Message

Methylation is an important whole body process that decreases with age and is also decreased by improper lifestyle and diet.

---

‡ Choline can be partially converted to TMG in the body, and therefore it is considered a methyl donor. Current reports indicate that only the choline converted to TMG is bioavailable as a methyl donor. Since this process is slow, the choline normally gets diverted to other functions in the body. In addition, Methionine recycles to homocysteine and while essential, needs to be limited.

IIX

METHYLATION AND HOMOCYSTEINE
(EARLY BENEFITS OF THE SEARCH)

Methionine is an essential amino acid found in many foods. During normal metabolism, methionine is partially converted to homocysteine, a toxic amino acid. However, in the presence of an adequate methylation system, homocysteine is quickly reconverted back to methionine. If this process doesn't work efficiently, homocysteine builds up in bodily fluids causing tissue damage and disease. This increase of homocysteine occurs with age, and is thought to be one of the harmful aging conditions that must be addressed in any anti-aging program. Elevated homocysteine§ is also an indication that optimum methylation is not occurring.

The diagram at the end of this section illustrates the main relationship between methylation and homocysteine. Under healthy conditions homocysteine rapidly converts to methionine or cystathionine, two non-toxic amino acids under normal conditions.

The key point to note is that homocysteine is converted to methionine (methylation) with the use of either TMG or with folic acid, and vitamin B-12. The transfer of a methyl group from TMG to homocysteine is done with the help of an

---

§ Each laboratory reports different numbers for "normal" levels of homocysteine. Remember, however, that "normal" levels are associated with high rates of heart disease, and "high" levels are associated with very early onset of heart disease. See Appendix on Testing Homocysteine Levels.

enzyme. The transfer of a methyl group from folic acid to homocysteine is even more complicated. First, a methyl group in the body is transferred to vitamin B-12, (hence folic acid and vitamin B-12 do not supply extra methyl groups), and then with the help of another enzyme and folic acid, the methyl group is transferred to homocysteine. TMG and folic acid are equal in their ability to lower homocysteine[6,7]. **For methylation, however, the pathway strongly suggests a larger role for TMG.**

Take Home Message

Homocysteine is converted to non-toxic amino acids, i.e. cystathionine and methionine, through the use of simple vitamins such as folic acid, B-12, and B-6. TMG is just as important as folic acid in this process. In fact, it will generally lower homocysteine when the B vitamins (folic acid, B-12, and B-6) are not doing their jobs properly. Research suggests that the combination of methyl donors including TMG works best. Most vitamin preparations fail to include TMG, the best-known methyl donor.

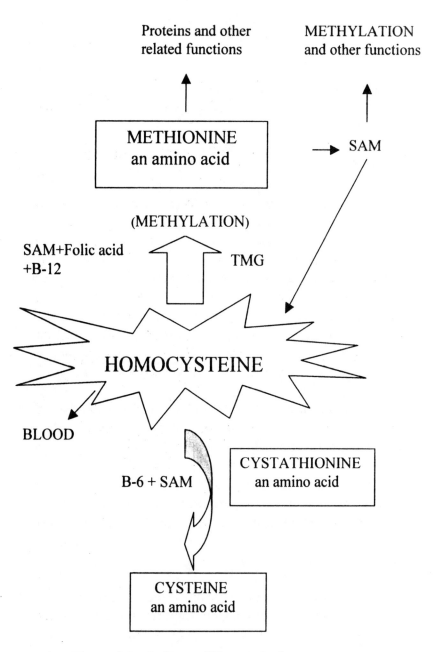

Figure: Metabolism of Homocysteine.

IX

SLUGGISH HOMOCYSTEINE METABOLISM AND RELATED DISORDERS

"Science is nothing but the finding of analogy, identity, in the most remote parts" — Ralph Waldo Emerson

Poor homocysteine metabolism means that the body is unable to quickly process homocysteine and produce the methyl donor SAM. When this happens, the body's cells have two problems: (1) excess homocysteine, which is then exported outside the cell where it causes vascular damage, heart disease, and a host of other degenerative diseases and (2) poor methylation, resulting in depleted detoxification, inadequate DNA methylation, and abnormal cellular activity, with implications in a large variety of disorders. These include spontaneous abortion, renal failure, arthritis, osteoporosis, and even gout.

Homocysteine metabolism inside the cell (as opposed to homocysteine in the plasma where it irritates the blood vessel walls) is extremely important. It is at the crossroads of two important metabolic systems: methylation of homocysteine to methionine and transsulfuration, which changes homocysteine into another essential amino acid, cysteine. Cysteine and methionine can then contribute to detoxification and a wide variety of other functions needed to keep the cell running efficiently.

High homocysteine levels in the blood indicate that these two pathways individually or both, are sluggish or overloaded with excess protein. In other words, they are operating, but not at the rate necessary for optimum cell function.

40

Homocysteine is toxic in blood and is related to elevated heart and cardiovascular disease risk. This in itself is enough reason to change your diet; however, because of sluggish homocysteine metabolism in the cell, diseases other than those found in the cardiovascular system can result. These include cancer, depression, birth defects and even impotence. The following table (Sluggish Homocysteine) lists some of the common diseases that may be related to sluggish homocysteine metabolism and high plasma homocysteine[2].

Table: Sluggish Homocysteine: Conditions thought to be associated with sluggish homocysteine metabolism[a]

Alcoholism	Osteoporosis
Alzheimer's disease	Parkinson's disease
Cognitive decline	Impotence
Coronary artery disease	Placental abruption
Deep vein thrombosis	Renal failure
Depression	Rheumatoid arthritis
Diabetic retinopathy	Mental disorder
Intermittent claudication	Aneurism
Multiple sclerosis	Cancer
Heart attack	Birth defects
Type II diabetes	Liver disorders

[a] Adapted from Miller and Kelly[2]. These conditions only touch the surface, as methylation and transsulfuration are global. Since aging is related to methylation of DNA and other functions modified by methylation, almost any disease may be related to sluggish homocysteine metabolism.

Methylation metabolism is critical for lowering homocysteine and maintaining DNA structure and function (low methylation of DNA is related to faster aging). However, methylation of other compounds and proteins in the body is also important. **There are over 100 different methylation reactions that take place in our cells and they are extremely important in the everyday activities of our body.** These reactions are associated with everything from detoxification (many toxic chemicals we are exposed to are made less dangerous by methylation) to hormones such as melatonin and epinephrine (adrenalin). As a matter of fact, methylation is involved with so many cell functions we could spend days and even weeks describing the methylated compounds and their importance to cell function and our health. **At this point, let's assume that methylation is related to cell function, how we feel, how we look, how we think and finally how fast we age.**

Homocysteine is methylated to produce methionine (see figure Homocysteine Metabolism). This is not the only thing that is happening to homocysteine. Actually two metabolic pathways are tugging at homocysteine simultaneously. At the same time homocysteine is being methylated, a portion of the homocysteine in the cell is being converted to other amino acids such as cysteine and taurine through an additional pathway which has been named the transsulfuration pathway (refer to figures on homocysteine metabolism). It was given this name because this pathway is important in moving sulfur from the amino acid methionine (through homocysteine) to other substances within the cell.

The quantity of homocysteine which leaves the cell and enters the blood plasma, where it is toxic, depends primarily on three known factors:

1. How much is being drained off into methionine (the methylation pathway, which uses TMG, folic acid, and vitamin B-12).
2. How much is being drained off into cystathionine and cysteine (the transsulfuration pathway which uses vitamin B-6).
3. The amount of methionine entering the cells.

These pathways will determine the quantity of excess homocysteine that will end up in the plasma. If we can speed up the removal of homocysteine through methylation and transsulfuration then less will be left for export into plasma. However, if insufficient methylation and/or transsulfuration is being carried out not only can toxic levels of homocysteine accumulate in the plasma, but other parts of the cell which depend on methylation and transsulfuration will be adversely affected.

In summary, three major activities associated with homocysteine are occurring simultaneously: 1) homocysteine to methionine (methylation), 2) homocysteine to other sulfur amino acids and 3) homocysteine exported to plasma.

It is apparent that homocysteine must be rapidly utilized. Conditions that allow homocysteine to back-up or accumulate will result in shortages of a variety of needed compounds, and dangerously high levels of plasma homocysteine. Inefficient processing of cellular homocysteine has been postulated to be involved in a staggering number of diseases[2], as summarized in the earlier table (Sluggish Homocysteine).

Many of the most popular nutrients sold in health food stores are synthesized in the body by recycling homocysteine.

We have emphasized the harmful characteristics of homocysteine. This refers to the level of homocysteine found in the blood, urine or other body fluids. However, when confined to the cells, homocysteine plays a variety of important roles. Like most amino acids, homocysteine is found in all the cells of the body. It is necessary for the metabolism of methyl groups and the transfer of sulfur. However, if methylation or the transfer of sulfur are sluggish, and especially if protein (methionine) intake is excessive, then surplus homocysteine is transported from the cell into plasma where it is toxic.

Inside the cell, however, homocysteine is the starting point for synthesis of a large number of compounds and proteins needed for a healthy cell. If a person could account for all the compounds and proteins made from homocysteine it would be in the thousands or tens of thousands. Many of these compounds have been found to be involved with maintaining or improving our general well being and health. One could look upon homocysteine as a starting ingredient in one of our body's many pharmaceutical factories. In this way, our body acts as a fantastic recycling center, converting the dangerous homocysteine to many essential nutrients.

The following are some of the nutrients that involve homocysteine metabolism and are sold in most health food stores: S-adenosylmethionine (SAM), carnitine (aids in burning fat), chondroitin sulfates, coenzyme Q 10 (helps heart muscle), creatine (used by weight lifters and athletes), cysteine (used as an antioxidant), dimethylglycine (performance enhancer), glucosamine sulfate, glutathione, melatonin, taurine, phosphatidylserine and phosphatidylcholine[2].

Figure. Sluggish homocysteine metabolism is related to many biological functions

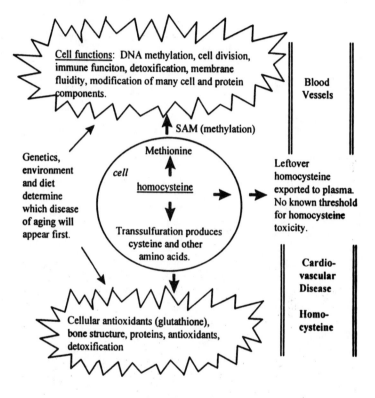

Cell functions: DNA methylation, cell division, immune funciton, detoxification, membrane fluidity, modification of many cell and protein components.

Blood Vessels

SAM (methylation)

Genetics, environment and diet determine which disease of aging will appear first.

cell

Methionine

homocysteine

Transsulfuration produces cysteine and other amino acids.

Leftover homocysteine exported to plasma. No known threshold for homocysteine toxicity.

Cardio-vascular Disease

Homo-cysteine

Cellular antioxidants (glutathione), bone structure, proteins, antioxidants, detoxification

It is difficult to overemphasize how important optimal homocysteine metabolism is to our general health.

We have, in this chapter, introduced the global effects of methylation and homocysteine metabolism. It is now time to get down to some of the specifics of the better known individual conditions and diseases mentioned.

X

THE HOMOCYSTEINE QUESTIONNAIRE
(WHO BENEFITS FROM THE EARLY DISCOVERY)

1. Do you exercise less than three times a week?

While exercise has long been known to help prevent many diseases including cardiovascular disease, there was no biological explanation until recently, when it was discovered that the risk factor known as **homocysteine** is reduced during exercise.

2. Is a significant amount of your diet derived from a box, a can, a bag, a freezer or fast food?

Processing foods removes vital nutrients required to maintain health. Processed foods contain a fraction of the critical vitamins, B-6, B-12 and folic acid. These nutrients are required to lower **homocysteine** and prevent cardiovascular disease. In addition, lack of these nutrients is related to carpal tunnel syndrome, anemia, polyp formation, rickets and a variety of neurological and developmental conditions.

3. Did anyone in your family suffer from premature vascular disease?

Recently, a genetic weakness in the body's ability to lower **homocysteine** has been linked to premature vascular disease. If your parents, grandparents, aunts or uncles suffered from strokes, heart attack, angina, or any vascular disease, you are at an increased risk for vascular disease even if all your standard risk factors are normal. Fortunately, researchers have discovered that betaine (TMG), combined with B-6, B-12 and folic acid, can prevent much of the damage created by this silent genetic defect.

4. Do you eat less than three courses of vegetables and fruits per day or consume a typical high protein diet?

While the benefits of moderate protein intake and an abundance of fruits and vegetables have long been advocated by health professionals, it is often unrealistic. Recently, the government reduced the recommended daily allowance (RDA) for folic acid simply because so few people were obtaining the required amount for proper health — not because the body suddenly required less vitamins. Only a diet high in fresh vegetables and fruits combined with moderate protein can keep our **homocysteine** levels low and allow for optimal health and longevity. In response to the reality of the American diet, the government has advocated using supplements in many foods, especially folic acid and B-6.

5. Do you eat commercial non-organic vegetables and fail to eat foods high in minerals?

Foods high in minerals include organic vegetables and sea vegetables. Both are common in Japan where both vascular disease and many of the types of cancer found in the U.S. are significantly less common. Minerals such as zinc and magnesium are required to allow the enzymes that lower **homocysteine** to function properly and maintain proper DNA methylation (described later).

6. Do you smoke, use birth control pills or consume excess caffeine?

Both smoking and birth control pills elevate **homocysteine** levels. Combined their effect is even more dramatic.

If you answered "yes" to ANY of the above questions you are at risk for disorders related to homocysteine and poor methylation, especially with regard to heart disease. Don't panic though: <u>Help is on the way!</u>

XI

HOMOCYSTEINE AND CARDIOVASCULAR DISEASE
(FROM THE HEART)

"Every heart that has beat strong and cheerfully has left a hopeful impulse behind it in the world, and bettered the tradition of mankind"
　—*Robert Louis Stevenson*

Without a doubt, the most common disease we associate with aging is cardiovascular disease. Cardiovascular disease is basically a disease in which the arteries of the body become damaged. More specifically, cardiovascular disease manifests as peripheral artery disease, myocardial infarction (heart attack), strokes, heart failure and aneurysm. However, the progress of most cardiovascular disease is the same. As an arterial wall becomes diseased, the artery becomes hard and thick, a condition referred to as arteriosclerosis. Atherosclerosis is the most common form of this degeneration, and refers to damage of the interior of the arteries, which allows smooth muscle cells to grow inward. These smooth muscle cells are combined with other connective tissue in a mass, called a plaque, which is a common first sign of cardiovascular disease. The plaque changes with time, gathering cholesterol and fat and becoming an atheroma. Eventually this atheroma thickens, distorting the artery, and calcium from the bloodstream accumulates in the lesion. This "hardens" the artery. As the plaque continues to increase in mass, calcification becomes so severe that the inside of the artery actually feels like it is lined with bits of broken glass, and the artery makes a crackling sound when bent. This type of pathology is obvious to the eye in most adult autopsies, and was noticed extensively in the remains of young men (18-25) killed in Vietnam, suggesting that cardiovascular disease starts much earlier than most people realize[8].

While the problem of atherosclerosis is systemic, and relates to the degeneration of the arteries in the entire body, it is often first seen in the heart or brain as most other tissues have a back-up system with other arteries supplying the same area with blood. When the atheroma blocks the blood supply to the heart, it is referred to as a myocardial infarction. When the atheroma blocks blood in the brain it is a stroke. If the penile artery is damaged or occluded, male impotence results. The kidney, retina and other organs can be damaged in the same way. Partial blocking also occurs as a result of arteriosclerosis. In the heart, the chest pain it produces is known as angina. Arteriosclerosis also creates weakness in the artery, and there are many conditions related to the rupturing or bulging of the artery wall, known as an aneurysm.

What Causes Heart and Vascular Disease?

Most people are taught cardiovascular disease is caused by dietary fats, dietary cholesterol, high serum cholesterol, elevated triglycerides, high blood pressure, smoking, genetics, lack of exercise, diabetes, birth control pills, gender (male) and stress. What is unusual about this theory is (according to Dr. Lewis Thomas, former President of the Memorial Sloan-Kettering Cancer Center) that never has there been any disease that has so many causes. As he stated, "Every disease that we do know about and for which we have really settled the issue, so that we can either turn it off, or prevent it once and for all — every such disease turns out to be a disease in which there is one central mechanism[8]." Corroborating his opinion is the fact that even when combined, the above causes account for less than half of all cardiovascular disease-related deaths, which indicates that there must be another, perhaps underlying cause.

The battle against cardiovascular disease has been largely unsuccessful because the focus has been on the above mentioned causes, particularly the concern about cholesterol. This failure shouldn't be too much of a surprise, because large scale human studies show that dietary cholesterol and blood cholesterol are mostly unrelated, and that feeding animals normal diets with the addition of high amounts of cholesterol does not cause arteriosclerosis.

In fact, mechanical damage to arteries, in the complete absence of dietary cholesterol, causes arteriosclerosis and the accumulation of cholesterol in the artery. While this evidence is old and unrefuted, the evidence in support of the cholesterol and lifestyle risk factor theory of cardiovascular disease (which is that low cholesterol diets, exercise, and a lifestyle change show a mild statistical benefit) created an industry directed at lowering these risk factors.

It is true that in shifting to a low cholesterol diet, some people have shown improvements in cardiovascular health, leading to the conclusion that dietary cholesterol and the other risk factors are the cause of heart disease, despite all evidence to the contrary. Unfortunately, less than 50% of the deaths attributed to cardiovascular disease are associated with cholesterol and the other risk factors, and simply decreasing cholesterol intake and eliminating the other risk factors from your lifestyle is not the real answer to preventing cardiovascular disease.

To summarize some of the major flaws in the cholesterol hypothesis:

- With no cholesterol in the diet plaques can be formed with simple mechanical stress to the artery.
- Large amounts of dietary cholesterol in the presence of a balanced diet fail to cause heart disease in animals.
- Dietary cholesterol and blood cholesterol are largely unrelated.
- Abnormal diets with one-fifteenth normal cholesterol can cause arteriosclerosis.
- Coronary patients had no anatomical differences associated with high cholesterol.
- Greater than 50% of all heart attacks are not associated with high cholesterol.

Dietary cholesterol is like a dragon. With so many people talking about it, one suspects that it is a real threat, and entire industries pop up guided by the single goal of slaying the dragon. This, of course, perpetuates the myth.

The most important point from a dietary perspective is the lack of association between dietary cholesterol and blood cholesterol. The following table supports this statement, and, furthermore, this table shows a close association between sugar consumption and cholesterol. While not illustrated in this table, most developed countries have both a high sugar consumption and a high degree of processed food, the later being associated with high homocysteine and both being associated with cardiovascular disease.

Country	Kcal	Fat (%)	Simple Sugars (%)	LDL+HDL mg/100cc
Korea	3.9	10.0	1.0	135
Uruguay	3.5	20.2	18.0	190
Chile	3.3	11.0	25.2	231
Spain	3.3	20.0	6.6	150
Venezuela	3.2	13.1	27.9	212
Columbia	3.1	15.8	24.0	165
Vietnam	3.1	12.9	7.4	140
Peru	3.1	16.1	10.8	138
Ethiopia	3.1	18.0	4.3	140
Burma	3.0	15.0	8.0	162
Thailand	2.9	11.1	1.6	132
Malaysia	2.8	18.7	11.0	173
Lebanon	2.8	17.0	9.2	155
Ecuador	2.8	12.0	20.0	192
Philippines	2.6	10.2	13.3	171
Bolivia	2.3	11.0	16.0	180

Adapted from Lopez, A., *Am. J. of Clin. Nutrition* 1966; 18:149-53 and C. Mudd, <u>Cholesterol and Your Health; The Great American Rip off</u>, 1990 (American Lite Company).

Cholesterol was mistakenly linked to cardiovascular disease because foods high in cholesterol often contribute to the real culprit, and that foods low in cholesterol are typically high in substances – the methyl donors and vitamin B-6 – which lower the true cause of cardiovascular disease. **The primary culprit is the damage to the interior of the artery, the main cause of which, as proposed by many researchers, is elevated homocysteine.**

Homocysteine is simply an amino acid. Historically, amino acids used to be considered a potential cause of heart disease. Many studies were done, however, which indicated that amino acids were unrelated to heart disease. Unfortunately, at the time those studies were done, homocysteine was not yet discovered, and proceeded to elude study with regard to heart disease for nearly 50 years.

Homocysteine entered the picture in the 1960s when Dr. Kilmer McCully performed pathological exams on children who had a genetic deficiency resulting in the accumulation of homocysteine. Since then, TMG has become part of the primary treatment for children with this condition. These children, when untreated, exhibited severe mental retardation and showed heart disease and severe artery damage that looked surprisingly like that exhibited by an older person with arteriosclerosis: partially occluded arteries and weakened artery walls. This observation led to the investigation of homocysteine and the theory that homocysteine could create damage to the vascular system[9,10]. Many studies were done, some of which are described below, and the evidence for the homocysteine theory of cardiovascular disease continues to gather support.

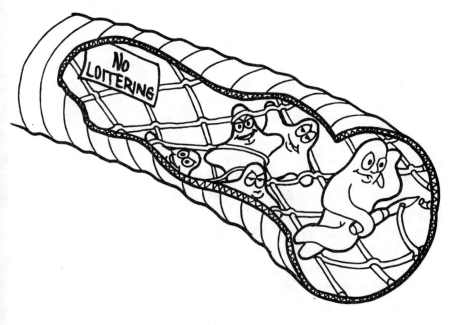

"Homocysteine molecules (the bad guys) are thought to damage the lining of the blood vessels and other important tissues."

It is now known that the most significant health problem related to high homocysteine levels is heart and vascular disease. Homocysteine is now thought to be the initiator in the cascade of events leading to heart and cardiovascular disease – as close to a single cause as one can get.

Unlike cholesterol, homocysteine passed the first test. When given to a variety of animals (baboons and rabbits) in realistic dosages, homocysteine caused arteriosclerosis. Quoting from Beyond Cholesterol: "Homocysteine rapidly induces the initial states of arteriosclerosis and cholesterol's effects are not apparent."[8] We certainly are not arguing that cholesterol has no role; in fact, it may play a role in the progression of heart disease, but it is almost certainly secondary to homocysteine.

Multiple studies have demonstrated that high and even intermediate levels of plasma homocysteine are associated with increased risk for heart disease, cerebrovascular disease and peripheral artery disease. Many of the key points from the recent studies were presented in the first section, "Quotes From the Medical Literature". The best known of these studies is the Physician's Health Study (the study that indicated that aspirin helps prevent heart attacks). In this study, researchers from Harvard compared the 5% (of a total of 14,915) of doctors with the highest homocysteine levels with the doctors in the study who had lower or normal homocysteine levels. **Doctors with high homocysteine were found to have 3.4 times greater risk of a heart attack than those with lower homocysteine levels.**[3] This increase in risk of heart attack (myocardial infarction) is comparable with the increase in risk caused by smoking – not surprising since smoking increases homocysteine. (This is only one of the many health risks encountered by smokers).

Many other studies have been performed which indicate that high homocysteine levels cause heart and vascular disease. For instance, in one study, 47 patients with peripheral artery occlusive disease had significantly higher levels of homocysteine than controls.[11] A study of 131 patients with premature vascular disease found impaired homocysteine metabolism in 28 patients (21%).[12] Several other studies demonstrated that homocysteine levels are increased in 15-40% of patients with vascular disease.[11] These include a study of 405 patients which found that those suffering from coronary artery disease had higher homocysteine concentrations than the healthy subjects, and a study which concluded that 68 patients suffering from cerebrovascular disease (i.e., strokes) had higher mean concentrations of homocysteine than 31 healthy patients. **It is clear that a main line of defense against heart attacks and strokes is to lower homocysteine levels.**

The good news is that we can lower homocysteine levels naturally, and thereby lower our risk of heart and vascular disease. In one study referred to above[12], daily treatment with the methyl donors choline, trimethylglycine, and folic acid normalized homocysteine levels in 16 out of 19 treated patients. In another study of 309 patients with premature vascular disease, 72 patients were found to have elevated levels of homocysteine, 66 (92%) of those who were treated with vitamin B-6 plus folic acid were able to normalize their homocysteine levels within six weeks.[13] In a case study, three patients with elevated homocysteine levels were treated with B-6 and folic acid for one month. **In two of the cases, homocysteine levels dropped, although not down to normal levels. When trimethylglycine was added to the treatment, homocysteine levels dropped to normal levels in two of the cases after one month, and in the third case, after three months homocysteine levels were reduced to normal.** In none of the three cases were any side effects observed. These results suggest that not only does methyl donor supplementation lower homocysteine levels, but also that using methyl donors in combination is more effective than using them independently. **TMG can reduce homocysteine in individuals that are resistant to treatment with folic acid, B-6 and B-12**.

Recent studies have shown that these supplements work best when used together. Not only do they lower homocysteine, but they help to maintain these low levels – with clinical verification for over a decade. A recent publication from Dr. Dudman and his associates at the University of New South Wales and the University of Queensland, Australia, showed this effect quite dramatically on subjects with massive genetic deficiencies[14] (subjects with a genetic defect in their ability to remove homocysteine on a normal diet). Considering the majority of cases of elevated homocysteine can be traced to nutritional inadequacy, the results are expected to be even more dramatic in the general population. If simple dietary factors (TMG, folic acid, vitamin B-12, and vitamin B-6) can alleviate conditions related to genetic deficiencies, with proven reduction in vascular disease mortality, consider how powerful these methods can be in the general population. It isn't surprising that recent data has shown a greater than 50% decrease in vascular disease in the sample of patients taking supplements.

Effect of TMG during long term therapy (in combination with the other vitamin co-factors, adapted from Dudman et al, 1996):

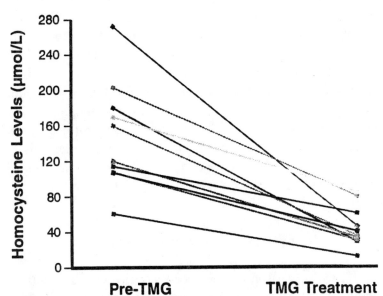

Plasma homocysteine before and during TMG therapy (concurrent with B-6 and folic acid administration) in patients with homocystinuria (deficiency of cystathionine β-synthase activity). Treatment for 9.1± 3.8 yrs in 10 patients.

Outcome of a Trial

Drs. Wilcken and Wilcken, from Australia, followed patients for a total of 539 patient years in 32 patients[15]. Without therapy, historical controls would normally have predicted 21 vascular events (pulmonary embolus, myocardial infarction etc.). With vitamin therapy, only two events occurred. **That computes to a greater than 10-fold level of protection against vascular disease in the population with genetically elevated homocysteine.** This data and the earlier quotes from the medical literature make it clear that homocysteine is a serious risk factor for heart and vascular disease, that it can be lowered, and this protects against vascular disease. This is unlike any other risk factor.

Homocysteine is not just a risk factor

Once vascular disease has been confirmed, survival is dependent on homocysteine levels (following figure). The most dramatic evidence for this was presented in the New England Journal of Medicine, July 24, 1997, by Dr. Nygård et al from Bergen, Norway[16], where statistics based on patients with coronary artery disease were used to estimate how survival depends on the homocysteine level.

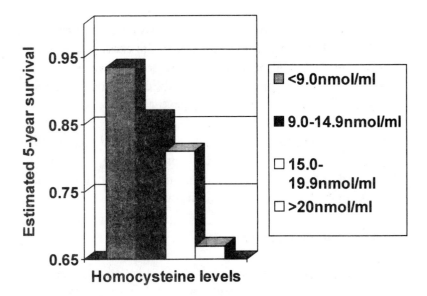

Figure: Survival after vascular disease depends on plasma homocysteine (adapted from Nygård et al, *NEJM*, 1997).

The preceding chart represents an estimated 5-year survival for a specified population (55-yr old male smokers with three-vessel disease). **The dramatic survival advantage obtained by having lower levels of homocysteine strongly suggests that homocysteine-lowering therapy can reduce the chance of future heart attacks and strokes in individuals with a previous history of heart attack or stroke.**

If you have homocysteine concentrations greater than 20 nmol/ml and you know you have cardiovascular disease, then it is imperative that homocysteine lowering therapy be employed.

In plain language, you're not expected to live very long if you don't lower your homocysteine.

Given all this data, homocysteine has only recently attracted the wide attention it deserves. As a result, the exact mechanism of action of homocysteine is still not completely understood. However, a recent peer-reviewed publication suggested that it could contribute to vascular disease through the:

"promotion of platelet activation and enhanced coagulability, increased smooth muscle cell proliferation, cytotoxicity, induction of endothelial dysfunction, and stimulation of LDL oxidation" –Drs. Duell and Malinow[17].

The authors go on to state:

"Levels of homocysteine can be reduced with pharmacologic doses of folic acid, pyridoxine, vitamin B-12, or betaine (TMG)."

Since we are suggesting that homocysteine causes heart disease, we would naturally expect that it relates to the standard risk factors. Unlike the other oddly unrelated risk factors, homocysteine relates quite intuitively:

Age is one standard risk factor for heart disease. When a child dies of a stroke or sudden heart attack, it is major news and the community mourns. When an adult dies of a heart attack, it may get mentioned in the obituaries, but does not command the same attention. This acceptance of heart disease in the elderly is the most telling sign that age is a risk factor associated with heart disease. Of course, the data verify this fact. Homocysteine increases with age, and methylation decreases with age.

Another risk factor is smoking. Normally, people are concerned with the "tar" in cigarettes, and worry about lung cancer. Rightfully so! But heart disease is also common in smokers, and this can be traced to the damage smoking does to the ability of the body to metabolize homocysteine using B-6. It is interesting to note that the increased heart disease related death rate for smokers is nearly identical to the death rate for people with high homocysteine.

There are risk factors that are generally understood to be "effects" or extra strains on the heart which, when the heart is damaged, can precipitate an early heart attack. Two of these include a measure of how overweight a patient is, and another is high blood pressure. More interesting risk factors, however, include lipoprotein-a, and fibrinogen, which relate not only to the plaque forming attributes of the blood, but also to the ability of the blood vessels to dilate, expand or clot. Both of these risk factors are activated by the presence of homocysteine. This was demonstrated by Dr. Peter Harpel at the Mt. Sinai School of Medicine in New York[18].

As a result, we can conclude that homocysteine is a killer. It is related to nearly every risk factor, can cause vascular damage, predicts survival in the face of already present disease, and ... is easy to lower. When it is lowered, we KNOW lives will be saved. It is possible that the mechanism of action will eventually suggest another more basic underlying problem, but at least we know that homocysteine is a risk factor, and that by lowering it, heart disease decreases.

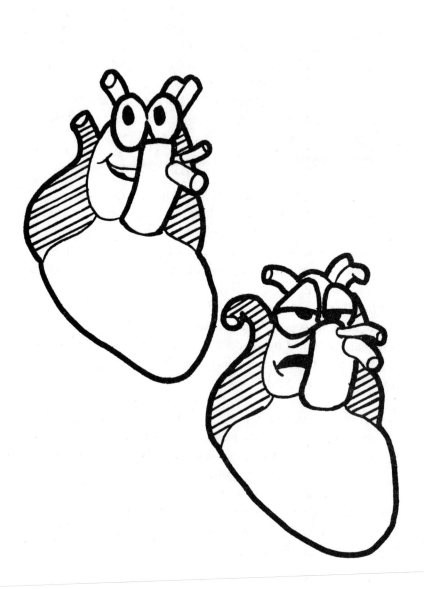

You may not be able to see your heart, but it certainly knows all your eating and lifestyle secrets. Keep your heart happy.

It has been conservatively predicted[5] that with proper supplementation, each year 50,000 people can avoid premature death due to heart disease in the United States alone.

Take Home Message

Homocysteine kills. Many studies and thousands of people have suffered to provide this information to you.

XII

HOMOCYSTEINE AND BIRTH DEFECTS

As women age, the risk of complications in a pregnancy increases. This is one of the most prominent concerns about aging in women contemplating having children. In addition to being considered by many researchers a causative factor in heart and vascular disease, **elevated homocysteine levels are also correlated with neural tube defects, as well as higher incidences of miscarriage -- events more common the older the mother.**

In a study conducted in Holland, doctors found that homocysteine concentrations in the amniotic fluid were significantly higher in 27 women carrying a fetus with a neural tube defect compared with 31 women carrying a healthy fetus[19]. Another study was done that compared homocysteine levels in mothers with pregnancies that produced 81 infants with neural tube defects and mothers with pregnancies that produced 323 normal children. Mothers of children with neural tube defects had significantly higher homocysteine levels than the mothers of normal children[20].

For many years, women have been told to take folic acid in order to prevent birth defects and miscarriages, and the reason for doing this is becoming increasingly clear: folic acid aids in the conversion of homocysteine to methionine. Thus, homocysteine levels are lowered, lessening the chances of birth defects. **However, both studies cited above showed that although homocysteine levels were elevated in women**

carrying fetuses with neural tube defects, there was no deficiency in folic acid. It is currently suggested that pregnant women or women trying to conceive take folic acid supplements. We suggest that this be done in conjunction with a series of homocysteine blood tests. These tests are extremely important, especially in high-risk pregnancies. If after taking folic acid (with B-12 both as a cofactor and to prevent the masking of pernicious anemia), homocysteine does not reduce to acceptable levels, additional supplements may be considered by your physician. These other supplements, such as TMG, have not been used extensively in pregnant women, so women are urged to stick to the well-studied and oft suggested folic acid unless advised otherwise by your physician.

It is also worth mentioning again that taking birth control pills can cause increased homocysteine levels, so that not only pregnant women, but any women on birth control pills who want to avoid the problems associated with elevated homocysteine levels, and enjoy the benefits of methylation should consider taking methyl supplements. Notably, in the Wilcken study previously discussed, the women with genetically elevated homocysteine levels (homocystinuria patients) were able to have normal pregnancies when using TMG and the methyl supplements – the only way those patients could reduce their homocysteine level.

Take Home Message

Methylation and homocysteine are related to birth defects. A simple blood test can indicate if a folic acid supplement is needed or sufficient.

XIII

OSTEOPOROSIS

Osteoporosis is a very modern phenomenon. Prior to World War I, individual cases of osteoporosis attracted a great deal of attention. Today, we use statistics to handle and analyze the large number of cases. This rise in occurrence is out of proportion to the increasing age of the population in the U.S. There is no doubt that osteoporosis has become pandemic. Since the 1950's the incidence of hip fractures has doubled in similarly aged populations, and forearm fractures have also doubled[21]. In comparison, cases of osteoporosis are still quite rare in the less developed countries, most notably China. Consistent with the story for heart disease and homocysteine and the admonitions against processed foods, Dr. Gaby[21] writes, in regards to the underlying reason for the increase in osteoporosis:

"The typical Western diet, with its high proportion of refined sugar, white flour, fat, and canned foods, contains far less of certain vitamins and minerals than diets consumed by our ancestors."

That diet and food refining lies at the core of many health problems was well understood by our ancestors – it wasn't just that refining was less common, but the medical leaders were more cognizant of the effects. The famous medical council to the Kings and Egyptian rulers, Rabbi Moses Maimonides, in the 13th century wrote:

".. fine flour sifted to such an extent that no trace of coarse bran remains. It is not proper to eat much of these foods."

Today the chemical brominating (bleaching to make the grain whiter) used in the processing of grains has brought "sifting" to a new low in the nutritional status of mankind, especially in the U.S.

This commonality between osteoporosis and heart disease belies further connections between the two conditions — the homocysteine connection. **In fact, people suffering from genetic defects leading directly to exceedingly high levels of plasma homocysteine and homocystinuria frequently suffer from osteoporosis.** In addition, there is a substantial increase in homocysteine levels after menopause, when osteoporosis starts to manifest. More than a decade ago, Dr. Brattstrom wrote in the peer-reviewed journal *Metabolism*:

"We speculate that moderate homocysteinemia might contribute to postmenopausal arteriosclerosis and osteoporosis[22]."

In the battle against osteoporosis, many doctors now use hormone replacement therapy. In 1997, two New Zealand researchers, Drs. Foster and Balfour noted that such hormones lowered homocysteine levels:

"Serum homocysteine levels were reported to decrease in postmenopausal women with high pretreatment levels[23]."

Such information is powerful, but the acid test is to give animals substances that raise homocysteine and study their bone density. In 1981, that study was conducted. Drs. Whiting and Draper administered sulfur amino acids to rats, and studied the effect on bones[24]. They administered a combination of

71

methionine and cystine (the former directly raises homocysteine levels). The results were dramatic. The rats femur bone showed lower weight, lower density, and lower calcium content. They postulated that this bone loss was due to the "decreased bone formation caused by a reaction between homocysteine and the aldehyde groups of collagen, as in genetic homo-cystinuric osteoporosis."

Calcium and other minerals are like the "stucco" in a house. They are added to the basic metal and wood frame to add support and stability. The proteins are the metal and wood frame, and excess homocysteine suggests an abnormal protein metabolism.

Further links between methylation and homocysteine and osteoporosis can be noted by studying the connections between zinc and B-6. Zinc activates SAM, and B-6 lowers homocysteine, and both are featured in Preventing and Reversing Osteoporosis, by Alan R. Gaby, M.D[21].

It is difficult for us to imagine any age-related disease that does not involve diminished methylation or elevated homocysteine. The collagen reactions mentioned earlier have been related to skin elasticity, and even tooth loss has some interesting connections.

Tooth loss is a terrible reality for many, and seriously lowers the quality of life. The initial deterioration leading to tooth decay is usually associated with early gum disease. Gum disease, in return, has long been connected to problems with folate metabolism, one of the key methods for enhancing methylation and decreasing homocysteine. Supplements containing folic acid have long been thought to reduce the inflammation in the gums[25] and mouthwash containing folic acid has proven to decrease gingivitis during pregnancy and improves the gums of periodontal patients[26,27]. Furthermore, many studies have noted that drugs which directly or indirectly interfere with the body's folic acid metabolism (calcium channel blockers, cyclosporine, phenytoin, nitrendipine, etc.) can cause serious gum disease, sometimes requiring surgery[28,29], and often results in premature tooth loss.

"There are many dangers associated with homocysteine. Stay out of dangerous waters by monitoring your homocysteine level."

XIV

METHYLATION, DNA, CANCER AND AGING

"The conclusion is made that the DNA methylation system may be considered as a genetically programmed mechanism for accumulating mutations during cell aging" – Dr. A.L. Mazin

All of our cells have exactly the same genetic material. We each have our own unique genetic code, more unique than our fingerprint. Lawyers use the fact that each cell contains the same unique genetic information to track criminals and determine fatherhood. Combined with the fact that our liver cells, skin cells, muscle cells, cells in the eye, brain cells, sperm cells, blood cells, pancreatic cells and more have exactly the same genetic code, is the obvious fact that the cells differ. A nerve cell might be several feet long and never divide, whereas a single skin cell divides rapidly and is too small for the human eye to discern – yet they have the exact same genetic code!

How can we reconcile this fact? Imagine a simplified situation. Suppose one cell is supposed to create a chemical that looks blue, as one might expect in the cells of the eye in a blue-eyed person. Suppose their skin cells are not supposed to create that same chemical, but instead are supposed to create a brown color that is typical. The same genetic code must be used for both cells. The way this occurs is that the genetic code that codes for "blue" and the genetic code that codes for "brown" are both contained in the same DNA (our genetic code). For the eye cells, the "brown" genes are silenced by covering up that section of the DNA, and for the skin cells, the "brown" genes are uncovered, and the "blue" genes are covered. In that way, one genetic code can create two colors. This process of "covering up" the DNA is usually done through a process where a chemical compound is put on the critical portion of the DNA, stopping that part of the DNA from being expressed. That chemical is called a methyl group, and the process of putting these methyl groups on the DNA is called DNA methylation.

Initially, when we are young, there are plenty of methyl groups, and genes are demethylated (uncovered) and used when needed. However, as we age, this pattern of methylation (what sections are covered or uncovered) loses its original pattern, and eventually genes which should have been covered get uncovered, resulting in cells which may lose their function, and in some cases, the expression of genes that can lead to cancer. This uncovering process has been verified in all mammals, and recently it has been shown that this loss of DNA methylation ability can be slowed by TMG and dietary supplements (Dr. Craig Cooney, aging researcher, personal communication).

As we grow older the methylation pattern changes and results in dysfunctional cells and even cancer. We see this change in cell function as aging. Diets that promote less than optimal methylation can result in gene expression or cell messages which make little sense to the cell.

Aging, as noted earlier, is change. If each of our cells did not change over time, or were replaced by identical cells, it is hard to imagine how the body could age. One of the most critical changes that occurs to the cells as they age is a change in their DNA and how the DNA is interpreted. Methylation patterns determine how our DNA is interpreted. In other words, if the cell interprets the instruction in a faulty manner it could be dangerous for the cell. **Methylation patterns change more rapidly as we age if we eat diets which lack adequate methyl donors.**

Therefore, besides the benefits associated with methylation relative to lowering homocysteine levels, methylation protects our DNA and prevents a variety of cancers in animal studies. By enhancing methylation, certain aspects of the aging process will be retarded.

METHYLATION OF DNA CHANGES AS WE AGE

Methyl groups stabilize our genetic messages when attached to the DNA in the proper places. A young person normally has more methyl groups than is necessary to maintain adequate methylation. Normal cells continue to divide as we age. Cancer cells divide even faster. In both cases, methyl groups are lost from the DNA during the cell division process, more so if inadequate methylation is occurring. The result of this loss of methyl groups from the DNA is inappropriate gene expression, which is implicated in certain cancers[4] and in the general aging process. The idea is that DNA methylation can prevent cancer-causing genes from being activated or at least put off the problem until you are older.

Many studies have shown that methyl deficient diets cause cancer in animals[4]. Furthermore, cancer cells appear to have a weakened ability to methylate DNA, which means that the loss of methyl groups is a vicious cycle: not having enough methyl groups encourages cancer to grow, and the presence of cancer itself suppresses DNA methylation. However, studies also show that methyl donor supplementation can increase the survival of animals with cancer and can prevent cancer in predisposed animals[4], strongly suggesting that methyl donor supplementation is a preventative measure against cancer. While there is at least one study on a genetically abnormal strain of mice which showed increased methylation increased polyp formation, there is little relevance to other types of cancer in animals or humans, and the vast majority of studies indicate that poor methylation is commonly associated with not only polyp formation, but other cancers as well. Once cancer has already occurred, however, some successful therapies are, counter intuitively, in direct opposition to this process of protection**.

The most commonly studied nutrient with respect to both methylation and its anticancer behavior is folate, or folic acid. This nutrient is found in cereals, liver, and vegetables. It was the ingredient extracted from spinach thought to explain the health attributes of spinach (remember Popeye?). In Cancer letters, in 1997, Drs. van Poppel and van den Berg, from the Netherlands, published a research paper entitled "Vitamins and Cancer [30]." In their review, they note that loss of methylation on oncogenes (genes which can cause cancer) can cause the oncogene to become active and result in cancer. They also report on some of the studies discussed in this section, noting that loss of DNA methylation has been observed in colon cancers. In addition, however, they note that folate deficiency, in a separate mechanism from DNA methylation, causes mutations in the DNA. This is due to the fact that folate is needed not just for transferring methyl groups, but it is also critical in the synthesis of DNA for daughter cells (daughter

---

** Methyltrexate, a common chemotherapeutic agent, interferes with folic acid. Dr. Burzynski's antineoplastons seek to reduce methylation to turn on some tumor suppressor genes or mutate the cell into programmed cell death. We have stressed that our program, like the government's plans to add folic acid to our diet, is designed to offset excess loss of methylation and is not designed to create excess methylation. We have also stressed the importance to consult your physician if you are undergoing any therapy or suffering from any disease.

cells are the cells produced after a cell divides – you hope they are identical). There is also evidence of low folate involved in abnormal pap smears. However, consistent with the lack of research on natural products and unpatentable nutraceuticals, the authors go on to note that prevention trials using folate in humans have not been reported.

One of the most exciting theories is that DNA demethylation offers a mechanism for the aging process. This helps us understand the cause of the physiological factors of aging, including the increased risk for a variety of diseases. In fact there are both theories and preliminary studies showing that methyl donors may be of benefit in the battle against graying, wrinkling, muscle slackening and bone density loss.

LOSS OF DNA METHYLATION AND AGING

The main thrust of the theory is that human beings have not evolved for extended longevity, but rather to reproduce and raise our offspring so they can, in turn, reproduce.[4] After this process is completed (usually occurring much earlier than we would like to admit) the scientific rationale for living is diminished. There is limited natural selection that directs our bodies to continue to live and we do not protect against certain types of deterioration – and our DNA becomes damaged. DNA is the blueprint for all cells, and it must be protected and maintained in order to slow the aging process. As we age, this maintenance, which requires methyl groups, is diminished. Essentially the warranty on our DNA runs out as methyl groups are depleted from the DNA. This loss causes a more relaxed control of gene expression, with time, altering our cells' ability to function properly. Therefore, in order to extend our longevity in a healthful way, we must enhance methylation in our bodies. This can be done through a combination of diet, lifestyle and supplementation.

The evidence for the DNA methylation theory of aging is very convincing. First, DNA methylation decreases dramatically over the life of all mammals. That is compounded by the fact that the shorter the typical species lifespan, the faster the loss of DNA methylation. This loss of DNA methylation is also able to explain the well-known Hayflick limit. In normal cells, after a certain number of cell divisions, the cell loses its ability to reproduce. This is one of the standard models of aging at the cellular level, and it is simply referred to as the Hayflick limit. In 1993 it was discovered that this aging limit coincides with demethylation – the loss of methyl groups on the DNA. That is exactly what Dr. Mazin was referring to in his paper entitled[31]:

The Loss of all genomic 5-methylcytosine (DNA methylation) coincides with Hayflick limit of aging cell lines.

Aside from the quote at the beginning of the section, Dr. Mazin reports that 39% of the original methylation pattern is lost during the aging of a rat. He goes on to state that DNA methylation **"may be one of the leading factors of aging"** [32].

In addition, accelerated aging, such as Werner's syndrome or Progeria, works through altered DNA structure. This alters methylation patterns, which has been proposed (personal communication, Bowles, 1998) to lead to accelerated aging.

Those diseases are related to a genetic defect which causes the DNA to unravel, failing to maintain the standard Watson-Crick double helix that is our typical picture of DNA. For Werner's syndrome that unraveling takes place after puberty and for Progeria that unraveling starts taking place during infancy. A picture of a patient with Werner's syndrome at age 36 looks like the picture of a 70 year old man. Progeria is even worse, with children looking elderly.

The unraveling of the DNA by itself does not explain the accelerated aging observed. What may explain the observed accelerated aging is altered DNA methylation once the DNA is not in the proper configuration (see figure DNA Methylation). Just last year, two researchers from the City of Hope in Duarte (one of the leading institutions studying DNA methylation), Drs. Smith and Baker noted that the ability of the DNA to methylate is stalled in the case of unraveled DNA, and this leads to a distinguishing behavior between unraveled and normal DNA[33].

NO ONE LIVES LONG ENOUGH TO CARRY OUT AGING STUDIES WITH HUMANS

Some of the above researchers were not theorizing about Progeria nor Werner's syndrome, but, instead were focusing on Huntington's disease. Anti-aging theories have one major problem. Unlike Methuselah, researchers have a typical life span, and like to see the results of their efforts while still alive. Thus, anti-aging protocols are hard to truly test in humans. Diseases like Progeria, Werner's syndrome and Huntington's disease provide valuable insight. In the latter case, patients who have the gene that codes for Huntington's disease live a relatively normal life until the gene kicks in. When the gene becomes functional and active, the patient suffers from tremors, neurological deficits and other problems that ultimately lead to early death. The question arises: what controls the timing of the onset of genetic expression? The answer. We don't know. However, there are some tantalizing clues. The first is to note that DNA methylation decreases with age, and that DNA methylation keeps certain genes from being expressed (even viral genes, see appendix). It seems obvious to study the DNA methylation pattern on the Huntington disease gene and note if lower DNA methylation levels coincide with early disease onset patients. Unfortunately, as of yet, no one has carried out that study due to the only recent development of DNA methylation studies and the identification of the Huntington's disease gene (HD gene). However, several indirect studies have been conducted.

As discussed earlier, the body uses methylation patterns to help determine which genes are active. In 1993, Dr. Reik and his associates from the Institute of Animal Physiology and Genetics Research in Cambridge, England, noted that there was loss of DNA methylation nearby the HD gene that occurred with age. They also noted that if the gene was inherited from the father, called paternal inheritance, that the onset was normally earlier[34]. Several researchers have hypothesized that this directly involves methylation:

Dr. Farrer, et al, Boston University School of medicine writes:

"The tendency for older fathers, including those not transmitting the HD gene, to have affected offspring with early-onset disease may be consistent with a gene imprinting mechanism involving DNA methylation[35]."

[Interpretation: DNA, the blueprint for our cells, sometimes has mistakes. If the blueprint codes for a defective function, one hopes that that part of the blueprint is not active, perhaps by being "covered up" with methyl groups. If the parent's gene was less "covered" the offspring's genes are more likely to be "uncovered" sooner, causing the cells to code for the defective processes that lead to disease at an earlier time. In other words, older fathers are more likely to be methylating poorly and because of this, they may transmit the early onset of disease to their offspring. We are aware that older women, probably because of poor methylation, have greater risk of producing

81

babies with birth defects. Now we are aware that older men may "pass on" problems to their children which may only appear many years later. Enhancing methylation may delay this effect.]

If this role of methylation is verified it will likely have a tremendous effect on a variety of conditions. For example, Dr. Chatkupt and his associates published a paper[36] discussing the role of genetic imprinting (how methylation and related patterns which "cover" the genes are passed from parents to offspring) and its relationship to diseases of aging. They explained that it relates to many other diseases including myotonic dystrophy, fragile X syndrome, spincerebellar ataxia type 1, neurofibromatosis type 1 and 2. They go on to state that methylation is one possible mechanism, and that this may have uses in the areas of clinical practice, from therapy to prenatal diagnosis and genetic counseling.

It must be stressed that we are only touching the surface. These rare conditions are all single gene defects. No common ailment is linked to such a simple cause. Cells work in networks, and typical diseases are related to disruption in cellular networks and are not traceable to single gene defects. Nevertheless, these rare conditions serve to illustrate the role of methylation in aging and disease.

The typical oversimplified image of DNA does not have the methyl groups displayed and does not explain many important features of DNA, nor how the body uses DNA as a blueprint for the cells.

Take Home Message

Methylation of DNA is necessary for stability of the genetic message. Methylation patterns of DNA partially explain why cells with the same genetic code behave so differently. DNA methylation patterns help determine whether a cell is a liver cell, a hair cell, a skin cell and so forth. As cells and thus animals age, methylation patterns change and allow different messages to be given to the cell. This change in behavior due to the loss of methylation patterns results in aging and sometimes cancer.

XV

METHYLATION IMPROVES ANTIOXIDANT PROTECTION

"Methylation is instrumental in the music that allows the cell to function"
—Fred Madsen

"Methylation and antioxidants act together as a shield against age-related deterioration"

It is interesting to compare methylation with antioxidants, which have had a lot of attention in recent years with regard to anti-aging. There have been numerous theories proposed on how antioxidants retard the aging process. These theories are based on the existence of damaging compounds and molecules that react aggressively and in a random manner with cellular compounds — free radicals. One of the most popular theories states that free radicals damage DNA (the blueprint for cellular structure and behavior) causing accumulated mutation and damage that can lead to cellular dysfunction. Failure to reasonably control this destructive process, known as oxidation, is now thought to lead to premature aging. Compounds that help control oxidation are known as antioxidants.

Methylation, on the other hand, is also important in maintaining DNA structure and function and retarding the onset of disease; however, by an *apparently* different chemical mechanism. Methylation modifies the structure of DNA and provides stability. It allows the cellular machinery (organized proteins and other biomolecules) to read and properly transcribe DNA (make the correct proteins so that cellular function goes as planned). DNA methylation patterns are influential in determining what messages are read. Different methylation patterns (remember that each cell has the same DNA) are critical in maintaining predetermined cell function. This pattern allows liver cells to be liver cells, heart cells to be heart cells and so on. Disruption or loss of fidelity of these patterns can lead to cells changing function such as seen in cancer.

The aging theory related to methylation[4] states that most cells have deficiencies in their ability to place methyl groups in the proper locations on DNA when cells divide during duplication. You need to continually produce new identical cells that replace older worn out cells to keep the body functioning properly. A drop or change in the methylation pattern means a change in the cell and aging. The less change in the duplicated cells, the less aging (see figure DNA Methylation on following page). Methylation deficiency allows misinterpretation of the messages in DNA, perpetuating changes that increase the incidence of disease and the signs of aging.

The theory suggests that one cannot consume enough methyl donors in a natural diet to substantially reduce the processes associated with normal aging. The "diet only" approach has been tried for thousands of years with no great success, especially in the modern era (although compliance, rather than substance may be why success has been limited). Instead, to retard this natural aging process, one would need to eat a diet that enhances methylation as well as supplement the diet with methyl donor nutrients at levels greater than could be accomplished with a natural diet alone.

Maintenance Methylation of DNA

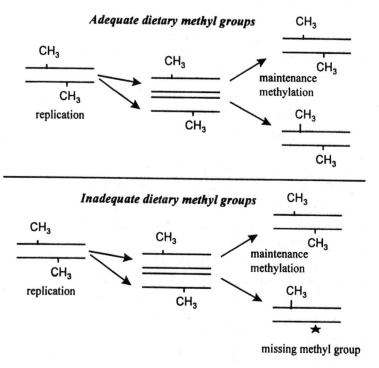

Figure: DNA methylation can be altered in dividing cells by diets with insufficient methyl donors. This results in changes in cell function, which leads to aging and disease. Note: DNA in divided cells with loss of methyl groups can provide incorrect messages to the new cells (adapted from a private communication from Dr. Craig Cooney).

When a person is young, this natural aging process (less than optimal methylation of DNA) is occurring even if that individual is eating a so-called healthy diet that maintains methylation. It is thought that additional methyl donors (i.e. TMG and to a lesser extent choline) need to be added to insure above normal methylation to retard this aging process. On the other hand, if a person is consuming a diet that is low in methyl group donors, the aging process on DNA will be more vigorous. When cells are young, the minor damage incurred by methyl donor deficiency generally causes little noticeable harm. However, by the time a person gets older (probably after puberty) and after many cell divisions the undesirable effects start to materialize. We generally start to see the effects of this accumulated damage by the time we are 30 (too soon for us!).

The loss of DNA methylation over time is analogous to loss of fidelity after re-recording music and can result in poor or improper gene expression and change the structure and behavior of the cell. The loss of methylation capacity during cell division is well documented, as is the random damage to DNA due to free radical reactions. The ability of antioxidants to reduce free radical damage (change) to DNA and the ability of methyl donors to help maintain DNA methylation are also documented in animal and laboratory experiments. Both antioxidant protection and methylation are important to maintain DNA integrity, which will translate into extended health and longevity.

What is Aging?

Remember, change, not how old you are, results in aging (wrinkles, graying hair, sagging skin etc.). If you can slow change you slow down the so-called aging process.

Change!

Antioxidants, antioxidant defense mechanisms (mostly protein and enzymes) and methylation share the ability to affect the health of the cell in a global manner[41,44]. That is because **these chemical reactions are involved in nearly every cellular process**. This "universal" relationship between general cell functioning and both methylation and antioxidants is critical for cell function and survival. Common sense tells us that we are not always privileged to be exposed to the best diets and environmental conditions. Therefore, the body has evolved to survive in less than optimal methylation and oxidative states. Our bodies can survive (although not happily) during periods of famine, drought, pestilence and all sorts of less than desirable environmental conditions.

Little or no research has been conducted to determine how much these conditions reduce life expectancy, but one would assume that they are detrimental. In contrast to starvation, calorie restriction can increase life expectancy[43]. The work of Taylor[43] was the first to show that calorie restriction reduces oxidative damage. Calorie restriction studies use diets with all known nutrients at adequate levels. The only change is reduced calories. It has been hypothesized that calorie restriction improves methylation of DNA[4].

Antioxidant defense and methylation are global. First let's look at how global antioxidant defenses work. Contrary to popular belief, the majority of the antioxidant defense system is composed of proteins. Therefore, maintenance of protein synthesis and turnover is at a premium when one is under oxidative stress. We are all familiar with the dietary antioxidants vitamin E, C, β-carotene and others. It may come as a surprise, but consumption of adequate amounts of dietary antioxidants play a small overall role in cellular antioxidant defense.

We have evolved a remarkably efficient mechanism to control cellular oxidation, recognize damaged molecules, remove the damaged molecules and repair the damage. The antioxidant defense system is composed of proteins, enzymes, metal complexing agents (chelators), metal-oxidizing proteins and antioxidant molecules.

The antioxidant defense system is composed mainly of proteins and enzymes††:

- Proteins that recognize damaged molecules.
- Proteins that remove damaged molecules from membranes and other cellular structures.
- Proteins which are involved with metabolism and degradation of these damaged molecules.
- Enzymes which control oxidation activity of oxidants such as peroxide, etc.
- Antioxidant molecules such as glutathione, uric acid, bilirubin, albumin, etc.
- Antioxidant molecules from foods such as vitamin E.

Most proteins in the antioxidant defense system are not directly involved in sacrificing themselves to save other more vulnerable proteins and molecules (the classical view of antioxidants), but rather function in the identification, removal and metabolism of oxidized biomolecules[1,41]. It has been estimated that a large portion of cellular proteins are involved in maintaining oxidation balance. In other words, control of oxidative metabolism (stress) is a much more important process quantitatively than most people realize. Protecting the cellular machinery from oxidative damage is a "big job" and a major portion of the cell is devoted to this effort. Most people think that antioxidant vitamins are "the antioxidants". However, in reality these antioxidants merely fine-tune the cellular antioxidant defense system.

---

†† It has been estimated that a major portion of the cell is involved in maintaining antioxidant activity. Many of the proteins in the antioxidant defense system depend on proper methylation for synthesis and activity. It is difficult to separate the metabolic events that are effected by methylation and antioxidant activities. In the overall scheme, antioxidants from foods play a minor role in cellular protection. However, they do fine tune the system.

Methylation is involved in the modification and building of many cellular proteins (no doubt many of which participate in antioxidant defense). Protein synthesis and cell division cannot proceed without methylation chemistry. Because of this, it would seem that less than optimal methylation or sluggish methylation could have a profound effect on the cell's ability to adequately protect itself from oxidation since antioxidant protection is dependent on abundant protein synthesis.

Antioxidant activity and methylation are interrelated and each depends on the other. A breakdown of either system can affect the integrity of the other. Adequate activity of both systems helps keep us from "rusting out".

Homocysteine may be a prooxidant. Homocysteine may cause vascular damage by oxidative mechanisms. Oxidative stress can also damage DNA, creating base changes that correlate with altered genetic expression. This is the classical theory of free radicals. Free radicals, however, can damage other tissues in the body. In particular, the current research indicates that homocysteine (in a special form called homocysteine thiolactone) binds to LDL particles creating LDL + Homocysteine aggregates. These aggregates are attacked by macrophages, part of the immune system, and the resulting reaction creates a free radical bombardment on the vascular tissue. It is this free radical activity, caused by homocysteine, which is thought to be the "why" behind the cardiovascular damage of homocysteine.

The human body is infinitely oxidizable as evidenced by the fact that only a handful of oxidized metals (ash) is left after cremation. Therefore, all the protein, fat, and carbohydrates of the body can be burned in air (oxygen) and oxidized. The cells of the body have evolved in such a way as to form a hierarchy of order of proteins and small molecules that protect the integrity of the cells from change or damage due to oxidation[37,38,39]. In other words, certain molecules and proteins can be oxidized (sacrificed) in preference of other cell proteins to maintain the function of the cell. Dietary vitamin E is such a molecule. It is oxidized faster than the membrane lipids which it protects[40]. An example of a protein antioxidant is albumin. Aside from other functions, it can act as an antioxidant by taking "oxidation hits" in order to protect other proteins and biomolecules. It is thought that the high methionine content of albumin is responsible for this activity[38]. Probably most would not think of methionine (the methylated product of homocysteine) as an antioxidant because of the many other functions of this amino acid. You have already read it is important in creating methylation activity through the formation of SAM. (Remember, however, that excess dietary methionine creates the toxic levels of homocysteine).

There are several approaches then to decreasing the vascular damage. First, lowering homocysteine. The second approach is to direct antioxidants at the free radical activity located at the cell membranes. This could possibly explain some of the animal studies linking lack of antioxidants to vascular disease. The only natural approach that is clearly confirmed to reduce the risk of vascular disease, however, is the lowering of homocysteine as discussed in this text.

Life is very complex and harmony among the many processes is necessary. Methylation and antioxidant defenses are both very complex and there needs to be harmony between these systems when they are combined into the larger functioning unit – the cell.

It is difficult to separate the metabolic activities of methylation and antioxidants. Adequate quantities of methyl donors are needed in the diet for protein synthesis, proper cell division, and maintenance of DNA integrity. The majority of the antioxidant defense system is made up of proteins. Antioxidant defense systems protect DNA, cell membranes and other cellular components including proteins. **When the two processes are combined, they provide a new and more powerful mechanism to protect the cell**. The strength of the new system is greater than the sum of the individual components. The entire group of compounds and chemical reactions work together to form a more stable cell chemistry.

This interrelationship between antioxidants and methylation is best observed by noting that free radical damage affects DNA methylation. This work, by Dr. Weitzman at Northwestern University Medical School and The Robert Lurie Cancer center, noted that in the development of carcinogenesis, methylation is altered by free radical damage – and that is thought to be one way free radical damage can lead to cancer[45].

In another publication from Moscow, Dr. Romanenko demonstrated that an antioxidant could result in rapid enhanced methylation[46]. Hence, one cannot ignore antioxidants or methylation.

It may be that a balanced diet (adequate in protein, carbohydrates, fats, minerals, and plant compounds), supplemental antioxidants, methyl donors and exercise will be necessary to maintain health and extend the quality of our lives.

Take Home Message

Both antioxidants and methyl donor supplements are necessary to maintain optimum cellular function. Both mechanisms protect the cell and decrease the opportunity for DNA mutation and cellular dysfunction. These mechanisms are important for health and longevity and their activities are interrelated and cannot be looked at separately. Both mechanisms should be evaluated in building a diet plan designed for health.

XVI

METHYLATION AND SAM:
FIGHTING DEPRESSION AND LIVER DISEASE

"The physician should desire that every sick person and every healthy person be constantly cheerful and relieved of the passions of the soul causing depression" – Maimonides, 1202 A.D.

We will establish methylation's role in depression and liver disease, but first we must discuss SAM, a product produced during the methylation process. The substance S-adenosylmethionine, or "SAM" is derived from methionine metabolism. Methionine is converted to SAM by the addition of adenosine triphosphate (ATP); a substance that is produced by our bodies naturally and is the primary molecular form of energy the body uses. **When methylation is working properly, homocysteine is quickly converted to methionine, allowing more SAM to be produced**. However, as we get older, this ability to quickly convert homocysteine is reduced.

NOTE: The nutrients that influence the clearing of homocysteine are interrelated. In this example, like with folic acid, SAM and proper methylation are necessary for maximum activity of the B-6 dependent homocysteine clearing pathway. One of the most interesting functions of SAM is its role in activating the B-6 pathway for lowering homocysteine. This means that higher levels of SAM improves the efficiency of B-6 in clearing homocysteine. Low levels of SAM and poor methylation reduce the ability of B-6 to lower homocysteine. This dependence of B-6 on SAM has been used to explain why supplemental B-6 does not always reduce plasma homocysteine when measured in the morning before a meal. This means that a balance of the key nutrients are important, and does not mean that supplemental B-6 is unimportant. To the contrary, the most accurate measure of homocysteine uses not only the fasting homocysteine level in the blood, but also measures how well the body reacts to a sudden increase in methionine, an amino acid known to increase homocysteine. B-6, while not significantly affecting the fasting homocysteine levels, plays a major role in the body's response to a sudden increase in homocysteine, which is dependent on proper methylation and high SAM levels. Whether this sudden increase in homocysteine or the total homocysteine load is more damaging is still unknown. SAM's role in activating the B-6 pathway only scratches the surface of the role of SAM in our body.

What are some other benefits of raising SAM levels? For one thing, SAM acts as a methyl donor for DNA, thereby protecting DNA, which as we already learned is a way to protect our cells from disease and aging. **Another benefit conferred by SAM is that it acts as a natural antidepressant.** A UCLA-Veterans Administration study[47] conducted with 15 patients suffering from major depression found that after being treated with SAM for 21 days, the patients who were treated improved their Hamilton scores (a standard psychiatric index for measuring depression) by 50%. **SAM, (which we know is increased by TMG and methylation), is successful in treating depression, without the usual drug side effects.**

Furthermore, there were no side effects with SAM, as compared to the potential cancer-promotion and immune impairment associated with certain standard antidepressant prescription drugs. For example, in a recent study, rodents given common mood-enhancement drugs experienced a significant increase in the rate of growth of cancers and an increase in the weight of tumors[48]. This result was observed with amounts that were consistent with the doses used in human patients. In addition, there have been over 21 *reported* cases of reactivation of herpes simplex or herpes zoster infection in human patients, suggesting that even a mild dose of such antidepressants impairs the body's ability to control disease. The exact opposite effects are observed with methylation, a process directly related to SAM, which is also an antidepressant (See appendix on AIDS and VIRUSES).

Are You Depressed?

There is a strong relationship between methylation activity and mild depression. SAM (the active methyl donor made from the amino acid methionine) has been used in Europe for several years to treat depression and other neurological disorders. If you have the "blues" or mild depression, this could be an indication that you are in need of a diet makeover and improved methylation.

"Methylation is important for maintaining a happy smile"

In addition, SAM has been shown to be helpful in treating dementia, which is particularly relevant to the elderly, who tend to suffer from age-related depression, which may well be brought on by decreased methylation capacity resulting in lower levels of SAM.

Methylation and the resulting production of SAM is an effective treatment in some cases of peripheral neuropathy, a nervous system disorder in the limbs and joints. In a case study[49], a 16 year old girl suffering from peripheral neuropathy manifested in the form of gait disturbance and muscle weakness was treated with TMG, the best dietary methyl donor. TMG increased SAM levels in the cerebrospinal fluid (which was previously undetectable) to normal levels after 24 months of treatment. Concurrently, she was able to walk again, and continued to improve with a methyl donor program in combination with prescription medications. In this case, while the primary cause was a genetic deficiency in methylation metabolism, simple dietary aids could undo much of the damage.

METHYLATION AND THE LIVER

Keep your liver smiling. Treat it with respect through proper
lifestyle and diet. It is a friend you want around for a long time!

Finally, SAM protects the liver from damage caused by alcohol. In a study at the University of Nebraska[50], rats were fed ethanol (grain alcohol) which induced fatty infiltration of the liver. Feeding the rats with TMG for four weeks quadrupled the level of SAM in the liver and reduced the fatty infiltration caused by alcohol. **This is partially due to the continued activity of the enzymes used by TMG to create SAM under alcohol stress. In contrast, the methyl donor folic acid has diminished activity in the presence of alcohol.** Recent studies from the same group at the Veteran's Administration Alcohol Research Center, showed that TMG not only enhanced SAM and countered some of the negative effects of alcohol in animals, but it also reduced the amount of triglycerides in the liver created by the excess alcohol. Dr. Barak goes on to state:

"In view of the fact that SAM has already been used successfully in the treatment of human maladies, including liver dysfunction, betaine (TMG), shown to protect against the early stages of alcoholic liver injury as well as being a SAM generator, may become a promising therapeutic agent and a possible alternative to expensive SAM in the treatment of liver disease and other human maladies" – Dr. Anthony Barak[51].

The way SAM protects the liver is also very interesting. SAM is used in the liver to convert phosphatidylethanolamine to phosphatidylcholine (PC). The result is an increase in PC and a significant improvement in liver function. In 1973, Dr. Wallnoefer, and his colleagues from Germany, showed that PC helped patients with a variety of liver conditions[52]. This included fatty degeneration, acute inflammation, chronic aggressive inflammation, and advanced fibrotic damage. In many of the cases the condition was successfully controlled and the liver enzymes (markers for liver disease) demonstrated significant improvement. Since that study, many follow up studies have continued to validate the role of PC in maintaining liver health. Dr. Parris Kidd, in summarizing the studies said[53]:

"The findings from numerous clinical trials, other human studies, and controlled experiments conducted with PC over the past quarter century altogether make a convincing case for PC as the single best validated nutrient for the liver".

Now we understand how to increase PC through methylation. It is also important to note that choline MUST first convert to TMG in order to function as a methyl donor and increase phosphatidylcholine. In fact, this step is typically very slow, perhaps explaining the less dramatic effects of choline in the liver when compared to TMG.

In addition to the studies described above, there have been numerous reports of beneficial effects of increased SAM. When given oral SAM directly, an 11-year old girl with MAT II deficiency actually watched the remyelination of her nerve cells on MRI. The liver enzymes of a patient with alcoholic liver disease dropped after treatment with SAM. Depressed patients improved 50%; Parkinson's patients noted less depression; Alzheimer's patients showed improvement as did epileptics, all after treatment with SAM. Clearly, a major benefit of methylation is its role in SAM production.

While the next figure shows how dramatic the increase of SAM is in a human subject taking oral TMG, it should be stressed that this is completely consistent with a near linear dependence of SAM levels observed in animals as a function of TMG dose upon injecting a TMG solution[54].

The obvious study would be to give TMG to normal patients and measure their SAM levels. Unfortunately, until recently the only way to measure SAM levels required a sampling of the cerebrospinal fluid, a relatively intrusive, dangerous and painful test (compared to simply taking blood). This is only done in research hospitals investigating rather rare cases. With regard to the TMG dosing, THIS DID OCCUR! In 1994, researchers in Japan were trying to help a 16-year old Japanese girl. She had high homocysteine due to a genetic disorder, with muscle weaknesses, convulsions, and other neurological deficits. The girl did not respond to therapy with folic acid, B-12 or B-6. They studied her SAM levels in her cerebrospinal fluids, and then gave her oral doses of TMG. As she improved they periodically measured her SAM levels. The results are summarized below. Now that SAM can be measured in blood (as of 1997), we expect to see a flurry of research articles studying SAM.

TMG and its role in SAM production[49]:

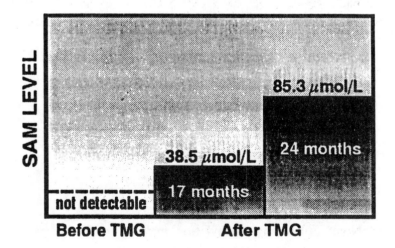

Application of TMG (after failed therapy with B-6 and folic acid) causes a dramatic rise in the SAM levels in a patient with homocystinuria.

What we then see is that TMG increases SAM, and SAM is an anti-depressant and benefits the liver. TMG has independently demonstrated its use in reducing fatty-liver under alcohol stress and in improving neurological conditions. ‡‡

Take Home Message

The process of methylation of homocysteine to methionine produces SAM. SAM is the major methyl donor in the body. It is important that we eat properly and supplement our diets to maintain good levels of SAM. SAM is involved in liver function, detoxification, mental health, protecting our genetic material and more.

---

‡‡ Note: Enhancing methylation may be inappropriate for schizophrenia or bipolar disorders. Please consult your physician for further information.

XVII

METHYLATION AND THE DIGESTIVE SYSTEM

Gastrointestinal health is important to maintain in order to live a full and pain-free life. There are many factors that contribute to our digestive system's health. One that is overlooked is the general state of the microorganisms that inhabit our digestive tracts.

It may surprise you, but there are more foreign cells (that is microorganisms such as bacteria, yeast, viruses and mycoplasma) living inside of us, in our digestive tracts, than the number of cells which make up our bodies (bacterial cells are roughly 1000 times smaller than our own cells). **A typical human stool is over 50% bacteria**. Biochemically, this mass of foreign cells is as powerful or more powerful than our liver. Kind of scary isn't it to think we harbor all this nasty stuff! Fortunately only a small fraction of gastrointestinal microbes is of a harmful nature.

We are all familiar with wine and beer brewing. Basically grains or fruit are added to warm water and fermenting microorganisms, in the case of brewing, yeast. The yeast start to multiply and digest the food into a mixture of alcohol and other material we call wine or beer. Fruit produces wine and grains and malt ends up as beer. Basically, because we don't fully digest our food, a process similar to this is taking place inside our digestive tracts; however, we don't have direct control over the exact nature of the fermenting microorganisms.

The main control we have over this process is through diet. The type of food we take in actually has a great influence on what type of microorganisms survive and flourish in our digestive system. In turn, the surviving microorganisms will determine what final biochemical products are made. It is beyond what we want to discuss in this book, but realize that the fermenting processes that go on inside the digestive tract have a tremendous impact on our general well being and our long-term health.

Each and every kind of foodstuff or supplement will impact this fermentation process. The effect can be small or large and either good or bad. However, the important thing to remember is that it will affect the microbial community within your digestive system.

<u>TMG influences the digestive tract in a positive fashion</u>. We have observed that farm animals and poultry supplemented with TMG have less digestive problems than animals or birds not given TMG. Animals and birds given TMG have more solid and well-formed stools when exposed to conditions that generally cause looseness or diarrhea. The common term used for this observation by animal nutritionists is improved water balance. However, another interpretation would be that they digest their food better and maintain a more stable microbial balance in the digestive tract (unbalanced gut microorganisms affect digestion).

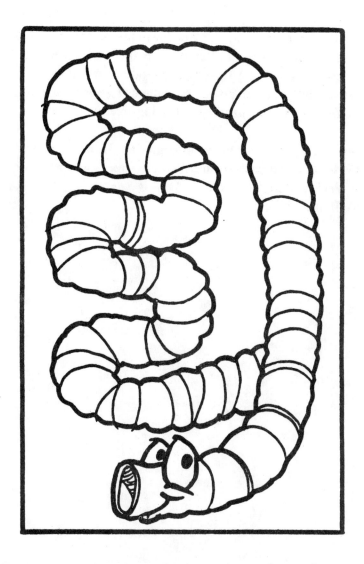

By proper care, the colon becomes one happy fermenting organ, efficiently removing waste, extracting nutrients, and creating needed compounds, aside from acting as a barrier against the nasty stuff in our foods. Keep the colon happy!

TMG has been in use by humans for many years now and one of the observations most often made by people consuming the supplement is that they digest their food better and have more consistent and uniform bowel movements (see appendix VI for more information on gastrointestinal problems).

Some TMG is present in the normal diet. However, we need to evaluate our health status, diet, environment and activity and decide whether extra TMG is something that will benefit our bodies.

XVIII

USING DIET, LIFESTYLE AND SUPPLEMENTS TO LOWER HOMOCYSTEINE AND IMPROVE METHYLATION

"Thou shalt not eat any abominable thing"
– Deuteronomy 14:3

There are many benefits of methylation. Helping prevent heart disease, cancer, liver disease, depression and perhaps slowing down even the perennial human condition of aging are some of the many benefits associated with the methylation process. **Lowering homocysteine, protecting DNA, and producing adequate levels of SAM are the three main ways that methylation works to enhance metabolic function and improve health.**

The question is: How do we increase methylation capacity to optimize metabolic function? Aside from taking methyl donor supplements (trimethylglycine, folic acid with its cofactor B-12, B-6, and choline, either alone or in combination), there are ways to lower homocysteine levels with diet. Most Americans are doing the opposite.

The standard American diet is filled with foods that increase the production of homocysteine and decrease the body's ability to remove homocysteine from the system. High amounts of protein, in particular animal protein, can increase the production of homocysteine (this means being extra-careful if you are taking protein powders or amino acid powders). Eating large amounts of saturated animal fats and processed fats such as margarine, contribute to high homocysteine levels (It should be noted that small amounts of good essential fatty acids, such as those found in fish oil, have actually proven to lower homocysteine). Diets low in folic acid and trimethylglycine, i.e., usually those lacking fresh fruits and vegetables, prevent the methylation of homocysteine into non-toxic amino acids. Eating processed, canned and frozen foods, which are low in B-6, and smoking or taking oral contraceptives, which further deplete B-6, also contribute to decreasing the body's ability to reduce homocysteine. In summary, eating the standard American diet of junk food, processed food, lots of protein and fats, along with taking oral contraceptives and smoking is a sure way to impair methylation metabolism and lead to an increase in homocysteine levels and increase the risk of homocysteine related health problems.

On the other hand, a diet low in processed foods, adequate but not excessive in protein, high in vegetables and limited in fats to moderate amounts of good fats - fish-body oil, and certain other vegetable oils along with avoiding smoking and oral contraceptives, is the most effective way to increase methyl donors and lower homocysteine, aside from taking methyl donor supplements. It is interesting that this plan is very similar to that of keeping cholesterol low, which contributed to the problem of obscuring homocysteine's role as a main cause of cardiovascular disease.

The prevalence of cardiovascular disease demonstrates that it is difficult to eat properly today. This is especially true in the face of the modern marketing techniques of fast food and processed foods —some of the least healthy foods in the history of mankind.

With regard to what should be eaten, mother is usually right! Eat your veggies! General rules: (1) select fresh organic foods: They have been shown to have up to three times the nutritional value of non-organic foods; (2) select unfarmed fish or free-range or game meats; (3) focus on vegetables and fruits; and (4) try cooking without oil (boiling, steaming, water-frying, blanching, etc).

With the synthetic compounds that are completely new to our diet, safety and health translate into abstinence. Unfortunately, we are rarely provided with the ingredients in anything we eat. Soft drink companies do not publish their formulas, fast food restaurants would never tell you what they put in their hamburger buns to keep them fluffy all day under a heat lamp, and the labeling laws have been written to allow for incomplete ingredient listing. One report notes that ice creams can have up to 100 synthetic products – some made from wood resin and others from industrial material. To avoid processed foods is to avoid these strange substances, aside from the benefits of maintaining food vitamin content.

Take Home Message
Eat unprocessed, organic foods, including plenty of vegetables. Avoid too much protein, excessive coffee, alcohol, and smoking. Fish oil and other unsaturated essential fat can also lower homocysteine.

Dinner with Fred and Paul

With the airport closed another day due to a horrific snowstorm, the authors were stuck at the airport in Rhode Island for an extra day.

Paul was facing a dilemma. He had exactly two homemade, vegetarian sushi rolls. Low in protein, high in organic vegetables, high in minerals due to the seaweed, and totally unprocessed, Paul questioned... Should he offer one of his rolls to Dr. Madsen, who was probably ill-prepared for the stayover? No. Fred would never know and Paul could enjoy both rolls, satisfying his desired level of nutrient intake.

Fred faced a similar problem. In his hotel room, he had blueberries, vegetables, tofu and the fixings for his special drink. His drink, with all natural, unprocessed foods, was his lifeblood and he didn't have any to spare. Should he offer some to Dr. Frankel? He figured Paul was probably ill-prepared for the stayover... No... Nutrition was too important and he would not let Paul in on his secret stash.

The phone rings. It's Paul. "Hey, what are you doing for food" (Paul, already having finished off his rolls, doesn't want to be anti-social.).
Fred, slurping down the last sip of his dinner drink, replies,

"Nothing. How about we meet in the lobby and get some food."
"Okay."

A few minutes later, they are standing outside waiting for a cab. Paul with pieces of seaweed stuck to his teeth, and Fred with blueberry stains on his shirt.

An hour later they are at the healthiest restaurant in town. The
waiter approaches:
"Drinks?"
"No."
"Appetizers?"
"All your appetizers are fried or fatty!?", retorts Paul.
"How about some bread?" asks the waiter.
Fred's face contorts and he looks visibly sick at the thought of
the commercial flour used to make their bread.

There is only one thing on the menu either would touch. Will
they order the same thing?
"Okay,... I'll just have the tea... do you have green tea?" ...

Realistically, the effort to eat properly in this day and age is
nearly impossible. We fight hard to maintain such a strict diet,
but we also realize that most will not be so disciplined. Even
though we both work hard to maintain proper nutrition, we both
fall short, and consume supplemental forms of methyl donors.

A combination of dietary and lifestyle factors seems to work
the best. Additionally, supplements such as trimethylglycine
and folic acid (with vitamin B-12, and vitamin E to protect the
vitamin B-12), and to a lesser extent choline, help improve
methylation and lower homocysteine.

XIX

TRIMETHYLGLYCINE (TMG) FROM BEETS

Ignored for its health enhancing qualities for decades, trimethylglycine (TMG) is still mostly used to increase animal performance and to flavor certain foods. It is made from sugar beets. TMG§§ is the newest and most effective natural methylation-enhancing nutrient. It is found in most microorganisms and almost all marine and fresh water invertebrates. **TMG assists the body in utilizing B-12, folic acid and B-6. It also helps the body lower toxic elements such as homocysteine and increases the natural mood elevator, S-adenosylmethionine**.

TMG is often referred to as a quasi-vitamin because although humans and other animals can synthesize it from choline, it can't be synthesized in adequate quantities and generally needs to be included in the diet. Metabolically, TMG is broken down into dimethylglycine (DMG) during the conversion of homocysteine to the non-toxic amino acid, methionine. A diet high in broccoli, spinach or beets can provide as much as a fifth or even a quarter teaspoon of TMG, just over 500 mg.

---

§§ Scientifically, TMG is a convenient designation for
1-carboxy-N,N,N - trimethylmethanaminium hydroxide, and is also called anhydrous betaine.

Where Does TMG Come From?

The process of extracting TMG from sugar beets does not require any solvents or alcohol.*** In its natural form TMG is a white crystal with a distinctive taste, which is sweet with a mild aftertaste. It may be dissolved in juice, water or tea. By taste it cannot be confused with betaine hydrochloride (betaine–HCl), which is very acidic, and will burn the tongue and the stomach. Several companies have mistakenly labeled betaine-HCl as TMG.

TMG is not the same as betaine-HCl. Betaine-HCl acts as stomach acidifier and is not practical in most individuals due to stomach irritation at the doses required to enhance methylation. Some middle-aged and older people should be tested by their physician to determine if they are producing adequate stomach acid. If not (a condition that could range from mild atrophic gastritis with hypochlorhydria to total gastric atrophy with achlorhydria), betaine-HCl may be considered. In that case, TMG can be exchanged with betaine-HCl on a unit for unit basis. Consult a physician if you have problems with bloating, gas or belching (see appendix for more information on bloating, gas and belching and the use of betaine-HCl).

*** A method called chromatographic separation– the best method, separates TMG based on its physical and chemical properties.

Chemical structure of TMG:

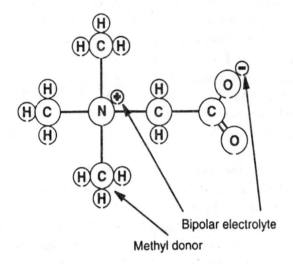

Bipolar electrolyte

Methyl donor

TMG is not unknown to the medical establishment. Used since 1981 in the treatment of homocystinuria (a disease caused by a genetic defect that reduces the body's ability to lower the toxic amino acid homocysteine), it has recently been approved by the FDA in the treatment of that disease. Sold since the early 1980's or prior as a supplement, TMG is actually a well understood nutrient, with no reports of negative side-effects when used in the usual dosages.

FOLIC ACID and B-12

Folic acid is one of the most powerful nutritional agents in the body. It is used for DNA synthesis, lowering homocysteine and much more. B-12 is also very important in converting homocysteine to methionine and should be added whenever folic acid is used. This avoids the possibility that folic acid could mask a serious vitamin B-12 deficiency. We suggest moderate doses. Some researchers[65] (Dr. Ubbink from the University of Pretoria, South Africa) have suggested higher levels of B-12. As people age, the level of intrinsic factor, a substance that helps absorb B-12, can decrease. Some medical professionals, especially in Europe, often supplement intrinsic factor in addition to B-12 for older people (note: supplementary forms of intrinsic factor are usually obtained from pig intestines). Higher levels of vitamin B-12 can counteract this problem through passive diffusion[66]. If you are over 50 and obtain the services of a physician trained in nutrition and have your vitamin status evaluated, an important point to remember is that "we are what we absorb and utilize" *not* "you are what you eat". Working together folic acid and B-12 are two of the best known agents for helping the body move methyl groups around for a variety of processes (they do not supply extra methyl groups such as is observed with TMG or SAM).

Vitamin B-6, and more…

Vitamin B-6 can also help by directly lowering homocysteine via an alternative pathway that does not enhance methyl group transfer. Optimization of this pathway is important to reduce homocysteine levels after eating a protein rich meal. Certain individuals may have trouble absorbing and converting dietary B-6 to the active form of B-6 (i.e. pyridoxal-5' phosphate). Therefore dietary B-6 should be provided in a bioavailable form so that plasma homocysteine can be lowered effectively in more people. In a recent study, it was found that over 40% of the patients studied had problems clearing homocysteine after a test meal[67]. Also, the European Concerted Action project[1] identified 27% of their test subjects as having difficulty clearing homocysteine after eating. The people in these two studies were at increased risk for cardiovascular disease because they did not clear homocysteine adequately after eating, even though their fasting homocysteine levels were not suggestive of increased risk.†††

In addition to B-6 (pyridoxine), folic acid and B-12, and TMG, other nutrients help ensure that homocysteine is lowered and methylation activity improved. The intended effect of the accessory nutrients is to maximize the synergistic action of the main methylating and homocysteine lowering nutrients. First, we suggest that pyridoxal-5' phosphate, which is considered the most biologically active and available source of B-6[68], be included as part of the B-6 supplementation. Biological activity of B-6 is particularly important to help decrease the daily homocysteine load for those people who have difficulty clearing homocysteine after a meal, but do not have elevated fasting homocysteine. Secondly, one of the main steps in methylating DNA is controlled by an enzyme that requires zinc for activity. Therefore, trace amounts of zinc should be included in the diet or a formula. The zinc we suggest, zinc monomethionate, is in a form that is absorbed well even in the presence of high levels of competitive inhibitors of zinc absorption (such as calcium rich or high fiber diets or possibly even folic acid). When supplementing zinc, it is usually considered prudent to include trace amounts of copper, as zinc is known to reduce the absorption of copper. Many people don't get their minimum requirement for either of these nutrients. It is also important to have adequate magnesium to metabolize B-6[69]. Magnesium is involved in the conversion of vitamin B-6 to the active coenzyme form of the vitamin. A

††† Excess vitamin B-6 can be toxic. Most people get far too little vitamin B-6, but the level should not dramatically exceed the level suggested in our guidelines without the advise of a health care professional. Balance is key, and disease can result by having either too little or too much B-6.

deficiency of magnesium could reduce the biological effect of vitamin B-6. **Magnesium is also needed for numerous methylating reactions, and in particular, the production of SAM**. Numerous surveys have suggested that most Americans do not consume adequate magnesium; therefore, to help insure the metabolism and activity of B-6 and methylating reactions, we often suggest supplemental magnesium. The particular form of the magnesium we like is magnesium glycinate. While expensive, it is far superior to magnesium oxide, an antacid.

Magnesium has several other roles related to cardiovascular disease. The most dramatic is the relationship low magnesium has with SUDDEN CARDIAC DEATH (SCD). Heart tissue requires proper timing of electrical signals for the muscle to contract properly. Magnesium plays a critical role in the electrical capacity of the heart. This is separate from its role with regard to homocysteine (which utilizes magnesium in the B-6 pathway and methylation reactions). The role of magnesium in sudden cardiac death was first recognized in population studies where a lower incidence of SCD was noticed in areas with higher magnesium concentration in the drinking water. The role of magnesium was further demonstrated when autopsies of people who died of SCD showed a low level of intracellular magnesium. Finally, it was noted that prompt treatment with magnesium could help prevent SCD[70].

Another nutrient that possibly supports methylation metabolism is taurine[71]. Taurine is an amino acid that is involved in a host of activities including the control of methylating membrane lipids. Reports suggest that taurine has a positive influence on this particular methylating process. Methylated and unmethylated phospholipids influence cell membrane structure, fluidity and metabolic activity. Generally, as animals age, the methylated variety of phospholipids decrease and the unmethylated phospholipids increase and thus the membranes are less efficient in their activities. The ratio of methylated to unmethylated phospholipids is influenced by a number of factors besides aging that include SAM, choline, essential fatty acids and taurine. Therefore, inclusion of some taurine may aid methylation activities and conserve SAM for other important methylating activities.

The methyl donors and homocysteine lowering compounds and their supporting nutrients should be taken at least two times per day in order to help maintain an improved methylation state and decrease the total homocysteine load.

The nutrients mentioned are in the realm of supplementation, and foods that are high in these methyl donors, such as green leafy vegetables and legumes, are part of a methylation-enhancing diet. However, it is difficult to even get the recommended daily allowances (RDA) through food alone. In addition, consuming quantities of protein which are more related to the body needs (most Americans consume more protein than they require) can reduce homocysteine levels.[72] Basically, the most workable advice to enhance methylation is to eat a well-balanced, organic and unprocessed diet high in vegetables, and supplement to ensure low homocysteine and proper methylation.

Take Home Message

Methylation can be enhanced by balancing the diet for protein, calories, vitamins and minerals. Most people consume too much protein and calories for their needs while not obtaining enough minerals and vitamins. This deadly combination not only works against methylation but also increases overall calorie consumption, which reduces the chances to live a long healthy life. We suggest some basic nutrients be included into your daily diet that will enhance methylation in most people.

XX

STRESSORS OF METHYLATION AND HOMOCYSTEINE

We have discussed the basic cellular and biochemical needs for methylation. However, **we must recognize that these needs or requirements are not static but change depending on our disease state or condition**. There are several conditions that may increase the need for methyl donors and they are listed in the following table on increased risk. Many conditions involve inflammation and this condition can increase our needs for dietary methyl donors. You may be surprised at how many diseases and infectious conditions cause inflammation[2]. It stands to reason that any universal biochemical process such as methylation which is necessary for all cells to function properly could be influenced by a wide variety of conditions or diseases. If you have a chronic inflammatory disease, allergies or any of the conditions listed earlier, you should have a blood test for homocysteine. The methylating agents described in this book may help offset the homocysteine-related damage accelerated by these conditions.

Table: Situations that may increase the risk of methyl group deficiency and increase the need for methyl donors.

---

1) Diets low in methyl donors, minerals and vitamins.

2) Inflammatory processes[a]: chronic conditions such as arthritis, infection (parasites, viral and bacterial), and acute phase response due to trauma.

3) Allergies

---

[a] Infections and arthritic conditions have been found to reduce the effectiveness of several B vitamins[55,56]. This may increase the need for methyl donors such as TMG to reduce homocysteine[57].

A point to remember would be that nutrient requirements are determined by several factors including sex, age, lean-body mass, activity, environment (toxic chemicals, temperature, etc.), disease exposure and chronic disease. Poultry scientists have been studying a condition called **immunological stress** for several years now[57]. There has been much written about this subject, and it is now accepted in all phases of animal nutrition. It **basically means that the presence of a disease challenge (organisms present that could cause disease or reduced performance) or disease causes the immune system (group of cells and chemicals) to become activated to maintain a safe environment for the cells and tissue. This activation requires biochemical energy and nutrients.** One of the nutrients which is needed in higher amounts during immune activation is methionine (required for some of the proteins involved in the immune response and also methylation for cellular expansion of the immune cells).

Weight Loss When You're Sick

Have you made the connection between getting sick and losing weight? If you have, you're right.

Most of this weight loss, primarily lean (muscle) tissue unfortunately, is due to activation of the immune system. Reduced food intake occurs but probably only has a minor impact on this loss. The activated immune system requires energy, amino acids and other nutrients for this increased activity. These extra nutrients are acquired from breakdown of lean tissue not fat stores. Methylation needs may be increased as a result of the activated immune system.

We are constantly being bombarded by bacteria, viruses and other infectious agents. Exposure to microorganisms and parasites raise the level of activity of the immune system. We may not experience a full-blown disease or illness but our bodies do respond to this constant harassment from these agents. This relentless battle raises the level of our immune system's involvement – high level of immunological stress with large challenge and low level of immunological stress when we are exposed to minimum amounts of bacteria, viruses, etc. **However, there is some level of immune stress at all times**.

Chronic diseases that involve the immune system, such as arthritis, elevate the activity of our immune system and may drain methyl groups from other necessary activities. The level of this immune challenge will determine the nutrient needs. There has been a lot of material in the animal nutrition press on how nutrient levels are changed due to disease and immunological stress; however, it is way beyond the scope of this book. What is important to remember is that many of the common diseases and chronic conditions that challenge humans no doubt affect our need for methylation. **Disease, infection and allergies probably increase our needs for methyl donors**.

Nutrient balance is important to animal nutritionists. Knowledge of the pathways involved in homocysteine metabolism suggests that there needs to be balance in the nutrients that drive the metabolism of these pathways. However, little or no definitive information is available to use as a guide to help make all the correct dietary adjustments. Animal nutritionists have been studying this subject for several years and may have some tips we humans can use.

Animal nutritionists are challenged with the goal of producing the best performing animals with the least amount of medication and feed. To do this they need an understanding of what nutrients are used for and what ratios and combinations work the best under a variety of growing conditions.

The nutrients methionine, choline and TMG are used by poultry and animal nutritionists to help meet these goals. Poultry nutritionists are probably further along in this process than the other nutritionists because they have larger numbers and less variable genetic lines of animals to work with. Much of the knowledge on how to use these nutrients have come from controlled experiments mostly performed by University personnel. Animal nutritionists, then have to take this information and make it work under the economies of commercial production. *In other words, it has to work or they get fired!*

Many commercial broiler operations today are using a combination of methionine (animal nutritionists look at total sulfur containing amino acids but generally manipulate added methionine), choline and TMG to obtain the best bird performance. In general they see better muscle production (breast meat), less food needed to produce the muscle, and generally healthier birds with the three ingredients than when only methionine and choline are supplemented to the diets.

They have found that part of the dietary methionine should be replaced by TMG to obtain the best performance. A portion of methionine, a rather large one, is needed for production of SAM. The majority of the rest of the dietary methionine is used for protein synthesis and other functions. Animal nutritionists have found that when they add nutrients in just the right amounts for their intended purposes it takes less feed (or calories) to do the job. Apparently, there is an optimum amount of TMG and methionine that produced the most efficient metabolism and therefore the animals need less food. In other words the bird or animal grows but takes fewer calories (this also has anti-aging implications: remember the studies on calorie restriction and its effect on longevity). The implication is that if you or I balance the nutrients in our diets more accurately, which includes methyl donors, we can reduce our daily calorie needs and improve our chances to live longer and more healthy lives (see appendix V for a table on the relative roles of TMG and methionine).

What do all these animal studies mean to a human? We cannot control our meals to the degree we do in animals; however, we can make some changes in our diets, which will tend to have the same effect. We suggest the following:

1) <u>Do not consume too much protein</u>. Consult a registered dietician and get an idea of how much protein you need per day. Next consume a greater quantity of your daily protein needs from vegetable protein. Vegetable protein generally has a smaller percentage of the total protein as methionine.

2) <u>Do not consume too many calories</u>. Animal research data suggests that better responses are obtained with TMG when excess calories are avoided. Also calorie or food restriction is the only repeatedly proven dietary technique to improve life expectancy. The more accurately you meet your dietary requirements without excess, the fewer calories you will need to maintain yourself. This, in essence, is calorie restriction.

3) <u>Supplement your diet with TMG.</u> Supplement your diet with between 500-2,000 milligrams per day. (This would depend on how large you are or how much lean mass is contained in your body. For instance, a small person of 100 pounds body weight with 20% body fat may only need 500 mg TMG per day, while a large man who weighs 250 pounds and 12% body fat may need 2,000 mg TMG per day. In addition, since creatine metabolism requires SAM and produces homocysteine, higher muscle content usually means higher homocysteine levels, requiring higher doses of TMG and related products.) Plasma homocysteine levels could be used as a guide to determine the most efficacious level of TMG to supplement (note: consult your physician to help you make this determination). However, if you cannot do this, 500 to 1,000 mg of TMG per day would be considered a safe level to take.

4) Folic acid, B-12, B-6, Magnesium and zinc are important nutrients to supplement and enhance homocysteine metabolism and the methylation processes.

History of TMG Use in Animal Nutrition

TMG was identified over 130 years ago as a component of sugar beet juice and is considered a safe ingredient for use in animal diets. About fifteen years ago TMG entered the U.S. animal feed market and has grown in popularity since that time.

Initially, it was used in swine diets to reduce the amount of body fat in market hogs and it has also been used in the fish industry to improve diet acceptability and as an aid to control water balance. TMG has been found to influence several other important economic parameters.

Recently, the poultry industry became interested in the unique properties of TMG as a nutrient. A significant portion of the poultry industry is using TMG today and usage appears to be growing. Economically important parameters that have been found to be influenced by TMG in poultry are: 1) better water balance (less diarrhea); 2) increased percentage of breast meat; 3) improved food usage and 4) better overall health[64]. Continued research into the use of the nutrients methionine, choline, and TMG is unveiling new insights as to how to better formulate these nutrients. Commercial poultry nutritionists are becoming aware of the importance in balance between the amino acid methionine and TMG.

Some of these commercial poultry operations process over a million birds a week. They have a large amount of data to make the judgement to use or avoid TMG. Each week more of these operations are using TMG.

XXI

A NOTE ON THE RDA

The RDA (recommended daily allowance) has nothing to do with the levels of nutrients suggested for the lowering of homocysteine. It has nothing to do with the optimal nutrients necessary for enhancing methylation. The RDA's for many nutrients have almost nothing to do with optimal health anyway!

The RDA for each nutrient is established by a blue-ribbon panel involving the National Research Council, the National Academy of Sciences, the National Academy of Engineering, and the Institute of Medicine. In 1980, the RDA for folic acid was set at 400mcg per day. Later, in 1989, it was dropped in half—

"primarily because large segments of the U.S. population failed to consume the established RDA of 400mcg." (Kilmer McCully, M.D., The Homocysteine Revolution,, 1997)

Such an *ad hoc* and unscientific method of changing the RDA underlies the fact that many nutritionists today ignore the RDAs. After that ruling in 1989, the Food and Drug Administration—

"ruled that sufficient folic acid be added to enriched foods, starting in 1998, to assure a minimum intake of 400 mcg of folic acid per day for pregnant women." (Kilmer McCully, M.D, see above)

This suggests that even the FDA realizes that the RDAs are insufficient for proper health in pregnant women. Similarly the RDA for vitamin B-6 was established without regard for homocysteine and the progression of vascular diseases.

Given that the RDAs are not the proper guidelines for the avoidance of degenerative disease, and were not even designed for optimal health, we have been forced to design our own guidelines. The guidelines are made with the following in mind:

1. The amounts should be obtainable by a good, natural diet. Providing excess nutrients is not supplementation, and is therefore not the subject of this book. Such caution is consistent with the charge "at first, do no harm", and avoids problems with individuals with very rare genetic defects (such as methionine adenosyltransferase deficiency or familial adenomatous polyposis) that might react negatively to non-physiological levels of nutrients.
2. The amounts have to be legal to obtain over the counter. For example, folic acid over 800mcg is available only with prescription.
3. The amounts have to be safe according to the medical literature, and not exceed values for which safety has been established.
4. The relative amounts must follow established guidelines. Where none exists, the relative amounts follow extrapolation from the animal experiments.

Table 1. Guidelines for Methyl Donor Supplements‡‡‡
People currently taking supplements need to be careful to factor in their current level of supplementation. To accommodate the fact that so many people are already on supplements, several companies have produced methyl products varying from just TMG to nearly all the of ingredients (guidelines adapted from Dr. Craig Cooney).

Folic Acid: 400-800 mcg (to be taken with or right after meals)

Vitamin B-12 (cyanocobalamin): 100-500 mcg

Trimethylglycine (betaine anhydrous): 500-1000 mg

Vitamin E (all natural vitamin E, containing a mixture of alpha, beta, gamma and delta tocopheryols): 200-400 mg

Choline (phosphatidylcholine, choline bitartrate): 0-250 mg

Magnesium (magnesium glycinate): 150-250 mg

Zinc (zinc monomethionate): 7.5-15 mg

Copper (copper glycinate): 0.25-0.5 mg

Fish-body oil containing DHA and EPA with 100-350 mg/g: 0-1 g

Vitamin B-6: 10-50 mg (~ 10%-20% from pyridoxal-5' phosphate)

Others: Intrinsic factor (pig derived product), taurine

---

‡‡‡ It is strongly recommended that all supplementation and exercise programs be undertaken with the supervision of a health care professional, and need to be modified in cases of mental disorders, cancer, Parkinson's disease, or in any case where active diseases are present, as some aspects of this program are inappropriate in certain cases. This program is intended for healthy individuals, and is not recommended as either a therapy or as a prenatal program.

Given the above guidelines, we developed a formula and tested it in a small group of volunteers. The formula has undergone several revisions over the past four years to fine-tune the level (remember, balance is important!) and every study suggests new adaptations. In particular, we are currently designing ways of tailoring the formula for the age of the individual.

The particular formula used in this pilot trial contained daily amounts of folic acid (800mcg), B-12 (cyanocobalamin 100 mcg), B-6 (10mg of a mix of pyridoxine HCL and pyridoxal 5' phosphate), TMG (1000 mg), copper glycinate (copper, 0.5 mg), zinc monomethionate (zinc, 7.5 mg), a mixture of choline bitartrate and phosphatidyl choline (choline, 100 mg), taurine (100 mg), and magnesium glycinate (magnesium, 150 mg). A total of 30 participants were selected on the criteria of having a high homocysteine level.§§§ The goal of the study was to observe the decrease in the fasting homocysteine levels in the blood as a result of the supplementation over a one-month period. There were then three blood samples taken, sample 1 – the screening sample and not done after an overnight fast, sample 2 – the pre-trial value obtained by measuring the fasting homocysteine level prior to the supplement, and finally, sample 3 – the fasting homocysteine level after 30 days of the supplement.

The results were dramatic. The homocysteine levels dropped from an average of 12.9 nmol/ml to 9.6 nmol/ml ($P < 0.001$). The results were statistically significant, with a probability of less than one tenth of one percent of it being a random occurrence and not due to the supplements!

---

§§§ It was interesting to note that the high homocysteine levels obtained from random blood samplings did not correspond very well with the fasting homocysteine levels later taken for the pilot trial. The fasting homocysteine levels were almost always lower than the screening values.

The results of the 30day trial are graphed below (data reproduced with permission from Dr. John Wise, et al, Personal Communication):

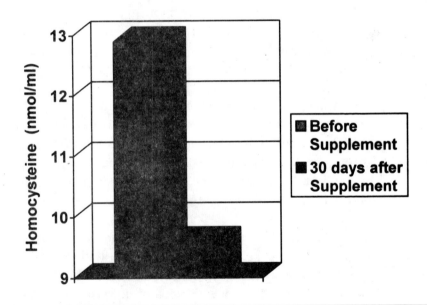

Homocysteine Pilot Trial

Legend:
- Before Supplement
- 30 days after Supplement

Figure: Plasma homocysteine as influenced by the methyl donors formula (presented two pages earlier).

The results are clear: homocysteine levels can be brought down quite effectively in a normal person (no genetic deficiency). With nearly a ten percent increase in vascular disease associated with every one point increase in homocysteine, the dramatic reduction in homocysteine could explain why previous studies have noted a greater than 50% reduction in vascular disease for people consuming supplements. While computations differ, there is no doubt that such a reduction would save lives. The only question is whether it would be 50,000 lives in the U.S. each year or more.

While such statistics seem cold, the fact that such a reduction in homocysteine levels would increase the chance of seeing your grandchildren grow up, or golfing your age, should not be overlooked. Considering that our sample of 30 volunteers were not even screened for a dietary deficiency (in fact, they were health care professionals and probably ate better than the average American), and did not have exceedingly high homocysteine levels, these results are truly impressive.

There are well-known commercially available supplements that advertise their ability to lower homocysteine. This formula, however, is the first to substantiate its ability in a normal population. **On another note, by using TMG, the formula is not designed just to lower homocysteine, but to enhance methylation**. Furthermore, in this study, some of the subjects were taking a well-known multi-vitamin, multi-mineral formula. **The formula succeeded in dropping the homocysteine levels substantially, even in people already using a standard supplement** supposedly designed to eliminate diet inadequacies (some of which are related to homocysteine).

We hope that this formula, or similar formulas, will soon generate enough commercial interest to fund a study on blood SAM levels, a new test developed by Dr. Craig Cooney and his associates. We know that SAM levels will go up, just as we knew that homocysteine levels would drop, but we need a clinical study on normal people to determine the average increase in SAM expected. That study will take considerably longer than 30 days considering the experience with the 16 yr.-old Japanese girl (T. Kishi et al), which showed a slow, but steady increase in SAM levels over the course of two years.

XXII

MORE QUOTES FROM THE MEDICAL LITERATURE

Lancet[73] (vol. 349, pg. 397. Feb 8, 1997)

"The present data extend the previous view that an increased level of plasma Hcy (homocysteine) may be a risk factor for CVD (cardiovascular disease)."

[Interpretation: The higher the amount of homocysteine in the blood the higher the risk of disease of the blood vessels or heart.]

Journal of Nutrition[14] (vol. 126, pg. 1295s-1300s, 1996)

"Long-term betaine (TMG) supplementation of 10 patients, who had pyridoxine-resistant homocystinuria and gross hyperhomocysteinemia due to a deficiency of cystathionine β-synthase activity, caused a substantial lowering of plasma homocysteine, which has now been maintained for periods of up to 13 years...We have found that prolonged betaine treatment, taken with concurrent vitamin B-6 and folic acid therapy, maintained its initial promise of lowering plasma homocysteine concentrations substantially in all patients."

[Interpretation: Even people who are genetically programmed to have high homocysteine and early disease can be treated with the same simple supplements.]

JAMA[74] (vol. 274, No. 19, pg. 1532, 1995)

"(the data suggest) that exercise, especially heavy physical activity exerts its most favorable effect in subjects with hyperhomocysteinemia.

Several studies have shown that there is a dose-dependent reduction in risk for coronary heart disease with physical activity, and a greater benefit has been demonstrated in older age groups. Since this effect cannot be fully explained by changes in other established risk factors, decreased plasma tHcy (total homocysteine) level may contribute to the beneficial effect of physical activity on coronary risk."

"...in patients with homocystinuria, the risk of a fatal thromboembolic event is substantially reduced after Hcy-lowering therapy".

[Interpretation: People genetically programmed to have deadly levels of homocysteine can be treated successfully with supplements. In addition, this risk factor finally explains the benefits of exercise with regard to heart attacks.]

Lancet[75] (vol. 346, pg. 1395-98, 1995)

"These findings suggest that tHcy (homocysteine) is a strong and independent risk factor for stroke"

"Moderately elevated Hcy concentrations, reflecting less severe genetic defects and deficiency of nutritional factors required for Hcy metabolism (folic acid, vitamin B12, vitamin B6) are common in the general population. There are consistent data from more than 20 cross-sectional and case-control studies linking moderate hyperhomocysteinaemia with

vascular disease, including peripheral vascular disease, ischaemic heart disease and stroke."

[Interpretation: Many people eat poorly, and fail to obtain the needed nutrients to lower homocysteine. This puts many people at risk for stroke and heart disease.]

Lancet[76] (vol. 349, pg. 1102-1103, April, 1997)

"Conversely, macroangiopathy at the level of the heart and legs is associated with clinical signs of microangiopathy, such as retinopathy and kidney disease. Thus, moderate hyperhomocysteinaemia may represent a mechanism that accounts for the concomitant presence of the two conditions in patients with insulin-dependent diabetes."

[Interpretation: Blood circulation problems are common in people with diabetes. This is related to high homocysteine levels.]

New England Journal of Medicine[16] (vol. 337, pg. 230, July 24, 1997)

"Plasma total homocysteine levels are a strong predictor of mortality in patients with angiographically confirmed coronary artery disease."

[Interpretation: Once the blood vessel supplying the heart muscle with blood is diseased, length of survival is shorter the higher the blood level of homocysteine.]

Alternative Medicine Review[2] (vol. 2(4), pg. 234, 1997)

"Elevated levels of homocysteine levels have been reported in patients with rheumatoid arthritis (RA)... Penicillamine, a common sulfhydryl-containing arthritis treatment has been found to lower elevated homocysteine levels."

[Interpretation: Arthritis is not only related to high levels of homocysteine, but one of the treatments for arthritis is a drug known to lower homocysteine.]

Alternative Medicine Review[2] (vol. 2(4), pg. 234, 1997)

"In children with homocystinuria osteoporosis is a common presenting symptom"

"...elevated levels (of homocysteine) could indicate nutritional deficiencies which might compromise function in virtually all phase II detoxification reactions"

[Interpretation: Elevated levels of homocysteine and poor methylation are related to many conditions, including those related to a toxic build-up of substances from cyanide to alcohol, and conditions as diverse as osteoporosis and heart disease.]

JAMA[3] (vol. 268, No. 7, pg. 877-881. Aug 12, 1992)

"Elevated homocyst(e)ine levels can often be normalized by modest doses of folate (1 to 5 mg/d). For cases that are resistant to this therapy, the addition of vitamin B6, choline or betaine (TMG) is often effective. These supplements at the recommended dosages have few or no side effects under most circumstances."

[Interpretation: **The leading medical journal produced by the American Medical Association has finally published an article clearly demonstrating the fact that vitamin supplements indeed work.**]

XXIII

A LAST NOTE ON HOMOCYSTEINE – The Ultimate Aging Molecule

"Eat Right *and* Take a Multivitamin"
—Godfrey Oakley, Jr., M.D.
New England Journal of Medicine,
April 9, 1998.

There is always something in life which is the biggest, greatest or most dangerous. The Titanic was supposed to be the greatest ship ever built. The great white shark is the most feared animal in the seas and Dirty Harry's 44 magnum was the world's most powerful handgun.

There are many molecules in the body that damage the cells and create a degeneration we refer to as aging. As with the analogy above, some aging molecules are more dangerous than others. We really don't know what the worst molecule in the body is at this point; however, homocysteine would have to be a strong candidate for the honor!

How could homocysteine be the ultimate aging molecule – the 44 magnum of biochemicals? Let's review a few important points on homocysteine metabolism. First, homocysteine, a toxic amino acid produced and recycled by all cells, can circulate throughout the body and damage the cells that line the vessels of our cardiovascular system. It can alter the structure of connective tissue in our hands, legs, bones and joints and may consequently result in arthritis and osteoporosis. Homocysteine can also change the structure of functional proteins in various organs which relates to many diseases that ravage our society[81]. It is readily apparent that homocysteine is toxic wherever it is found.

In addition, homocysteine metabolism is closely related to methylation ability. Specifically, high homocysteine is linked with poor methylation. Reduced methylation ability may be one of the primary causes of aging. Fast aging animals lose methylation on their DNA faster than slower aging animals, and the aging of cells known as the Hayflick limit is linked to poor methylation.

We are not aware of any other aging molecule that is connected to so many diseases. Homocysteine has been scientifically linked to Alzheimer's disease, cognitive decline, coronary artery disease, depression, diabetic retinopathy, multiple sclerosis, heart attack, diabetes, osteoporosis, Parkinson's disease, renal failure, rheumatoid arthritis, cancer and liver disorders. It is difficult for us to imagine any age related disease that does not involve impaired methylation or elevated homocysteine.

Homocysteine and methylation are related to how we look, how we feel, think, and finally, how fast we age and die. Homocysteine may truly be the ultimate aging molecule.

APPENDIX I METHYLATION, FATS, DRUGS, AND VIRUSES

Methionine, trimethylglycine (TMG), and choline are referred to as lipotropic substances for their ability to alter fat metabolism. Trimethylglycine, the best known methyl donor (methionine is also technically a methyl donor, but trimethylglycine is 2.3 times more effective and doesn't have the side effect of increasing homocysteine levels) has interesting effects on fat and muscle behavior. In animals, trimethylglycine decreases VLDLs, increases muscle mass, and decreases fat content. Trimethylglycine is also known to increase bone density. These effects are poorly understood, but well documented. We do know, however, that such results are only obtainable when controlling calorie intake.

In addition, trimethylglycine becomes dimethylglycine after donating one methyl group to convert homocysteine to methionine. Dimethylglycine, or its related compound, vitamin B-15, the first performance enhancer sold in the United States, was extensively used by athletes in the former Soviet Union and remains a popular item in most health food stores. It was shown that trimethylglycine dramatically increases the level of dimethylglycine as a result of the catabolism of the trimethylglycine in the methyl donation process.

METHYL DONORS, DRUG INTERACTIONS AND ADDITIONAL INFORMATION

There are a few studies of drug interactions with the methyl donors. Specifically, folic acid is often avoided in patients receiving certain types of chemotherapy. Another report showed that animals given trimethylglycine in addition to antibiotics recovered faster and had less diarrhea. Trimethylglycine is currently being studied for its beneficial effects in colon health and regularity. In addition to its methyl donation ability, trimethylglycine is an osmoprotectant, which is thought to benefit digestion. This is a different action than that of betaine HCl, a stomach acidifier.

The suggested amount of TMG given in Table 1 is approximately how much TMG one would obtain by eating a diet with a large amount of broccoli or beets. There are no reports of any adverse side effects with TMG. Like choline, however, TMG can cause a brief muscle-tension headache if taken in large quantities without food. In addition, newcomers to the methyl program should start off with no more than 500 mg per day of TMG.

THE AIDS AND VIRAL CONNECTION

The relation of homocysteine metabolism and AIDS is not clear. What is clear is that in AIDS patients a very reactive form of homocysteine is at a level significantly higher than in normal people. This was reported at a recent homocysteine conference. In particular, Drs. Müller and Ueland and their associates from Norway found that certain forms of homocysteine were approximately 3 times higher. In addition, AIDS dementia (occurring in 30% of HIV-infected patients) is associated with low levels of SAM in the cerebrospinal fluid. It is hoped that, as in the case of the 16-year old girl suffering from peripheral neuropathy, the level of SAM can be increased by methyl supplements, and, as in her case, that the symptoms will improve.

The viral story is not just related to homocysteine. When viral genes are inserted in cells, including the genes for the herpes simplex virus, adenovirus 2, mouse mammary tumor virus, Moloney murine leukemia virus, and more, unmethylated DNA is transformed much more efficiently than methylated DNA.

These viruses are retroviruses, which means that they are small sections of genetic code that incorporate themselves into the human cell's DNA, and use the human cell's own machinery to make duplicate copies. Just as DNA methylation can "cover" up undesirable genes such as cancer genes, DNA methylation can apparently "cover" up the viral genes, reducing the cells' production of viral particles. Further, lower DNA methylation is associated with higher virus expression in avian sarcoma virus, mouse endogenous type C virus, mammary tumor viruses, herpes simplex virus, herpes saimiri virus, Epstein-Barr virus, marek's disease virus, and AKR murine leukemia virus.

This lead naturally to the study of DNA methylation and the latency of HIV-1. Published in 1990 from Johns Hopkins by Drs. Bednarik, Cook and Pitha, the HIV LTR sequence was SILENCED by hypermethylation in vitro. It was reactivated by demethylation. In human cells, virus production was only observed after demethylation with 5-azacytidine or irradiation. Clearly, given the ability of proper dietary supplements to remethylate DNA, it won't be long before a clinical trial will be conducted. It should be noted that while the loss of DNA methylation with age can cause many problems, it is theoretically possible to over compensate, causing the methylation of genes that one wants expressed. Too much of nearly anything can be detrimental, and such "balance" and the exact effects of methylation over the large genetic variation of people suggests many in depth studies. This has, of course, been delayed, as most research does not focus on natural dietary ingredients, but instead had focused on the triple therapies produced by patentable technologies.

Herpes Eruptions May Be Another Reason to Consider TMG

A significant portion of the population now has either oral or genital herpes. The viruses that cause these painful eruptions lie dormant inside the cells DNA (cell's genetic blueprint) until a stressful event causes the virus to be produced and results in the painful episodes so familiar to people that have the disease.

Methyl groups in sufficient quantity may reduce the number of these episodes. Methyl groups properly placed on DNA (this means in the right place and correct amount) are thought to keep certain viruses and virus-like particles from being expressed (become active)[58,59,60,61]. During periods of low methylation (low nutrient intake, immune stress which increases methyl group demand, becoming run down), viruses (in this case the herpes virus) present in the cell's DNA can become active. Keeping the cell's DNA methylated sufficiently may keep herpes and other viruses associated with DNA silent (you still have the virus, but it doesn't cause disease and pain).

APPENDIX II TESTING HOMOCYSTEINE LEVELS

Homocysteine levels in the blood can be checked in the morning, prior to eating. The blood must be processed immediately according to the directions included at the end of this section as letting the blood sit for even a few minutes at room temperature will release homocysteine from the red blood cells and confound the results. Levels above 16 nmol/mL (average is approximately 10 nmol/mL) should prompt action with diet, lifestyle and supplements. Women should be even more careful.

Tests taken without fasting will usually be higher, and should be avoided. The homocysteine test is a fairly sophisticated test, requiring substantial processing at the laboratory. (Specialty is the laboratory suggested to the authors by Dr. Kilmer McCully, the originator of the homocysteine theory of heart disease).

Tests for B-6 (pyridoxine) enzymes can also be of value as a B-6 deficiency will cause elevated homocysteine in a methionine loading test, but not always in a fasting homocysteine test.

Ultimately, for those with a family history of premature vascular disease, a methionine-loading test should be conducted to rule out heterozygosity for cystathionine β-synthase deficiency. These decisions and tests should be made and performed with your doctor.

Elevated blood levels of fibrinogen (a component of the blood clotting mechanism) and/or Lipoprotein (a) in the presence of elevated homocysteine, also increase the risk of cardiovascular disease and stroke.

TEST ORDERING INFORMATION
(800) 344-1845

Please note that the following tests available from Specialty Laboratories must be ordered by a physician. Courier pickup services are available in most major metropolitan areas.

Thrombotic Risk AssessR™   code #5990
Fibrinogen
Homocysteine UltraQuant™
Lipoprotein (a) [Lp(a)]
Specimen Requirements: **Two** 1 mL aliquots of citrated, platelet-poor plasma, ship **FROZEN**.

Treatable Ischemia PredictR™ (TIP)   code #1537
C-Reactive Protein UltraQuant™
Homocysteine UltraQuant™
C. pneumoniae Antibodies UltraQuant™
Specimen Requirements: 5 mL EDTA plasma, ship ambient, refrigerated, or frozen.

Venous Thromboembolism (VTE) AssessR™ code #5975
Factor V Mutation (Leiden)
Homocysteine UltraQuant™
Specimen Requirements: 5 mL whole blood EDTA, AMBIENT, and 2 mL serum, ambient, refrigerated or frozen.

Megaloblastic Anemia AssessR™   code #4994
Homocysteine UltraQuant™
Methylmalonic Acid
Specimen Requirements: 3 mL serum, ship **FROZEN**.

Homocysteine UltraQuant™   code #3334
Specimen Requirements: **Two** 1 mL aliquots of serum or
plasma, ship ambient, refrigerated, or frozen.

Fibrinogen (Test code #1426) and **Lipoprotein (a) [Lp(a)]**
(Test code #3446) also available individually.

Folate (Folic Acid)   code #3522
Specimen Requirements: 2 mL unhemolyzed serum, ship
refrigerated.

Methylmalonic Acid   code #3496
Specimen Requirements: 3 mL serum, ship refrigerated or
frozen.

To receive additional information about the homocysteine
tests or for ordering information please call (800) 344-1845.

Specialty Laboratories
2211 Michigan Avenue
Santa Monica, CA 90404-3900
http://www.specialtylabs.com

APPENDIX III PERFORMANCE

With a special report by Dr. James Lembeck, noted author on athletic performance.

From Kipling's Mowgli, to Tarzan and even George of the Jungle, plenty of exercise and a good natural diet have long been associated with strength, vigor and endurance.

Dr. James Lembeck performed an informal four-week study with 30 subjects who performed aerobic and anaerobic types of exercise using TMG properly balanced with other nutrients to enhance performance. The subjects were not told what they were taking nor why they were taking it, only that they needed to use the product twice daily first thing in the morning and just prior to exercise. The subjects were also asked to stop taking certain other supplements for the duration of the study. Of the test subjects that finished the study, **92% felt that their energy levels had significantly increased while others felt a moderate increase in energy. Those that weight trained reported dramatic increases in weight-lifts and felt they recuperated faster. Almost all of the endurance athletes described increased ability to work longer, and felt they had energy to spare.** These results are not scientific; they are just an indicator that a TMG based formulation when used by regular athletes may have the potential to increase athletic performance on several levels. As funding becomes available more rigorous types of testing can be employed to obtain additional information for the different types of athletes that would benefit from the use of TMG in properly balanced formulations.

The following table represents the percentage of athletes who completed the study and reported significant improvement in subjective measurements of the performance aspects of a TMG based athletic product.

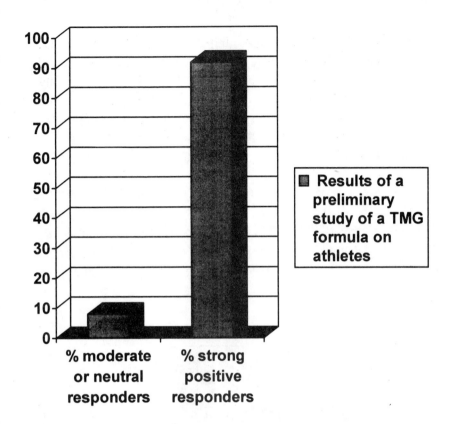

Figure: Percentage of athletes that responded favorably to TMG supplementation.

This preliminary human study is a natural step following the animal studies. The first of these animal studies was conducted on salmon, where TMG was able to promote better meat quality (decreased fatty meat) and increased resistance to changes in the amount of salt in the water (osmotic changes). For that industry, TMG has become a standard feed additive. That was quickly followed by studies on other farm animals, especially chickens and pigs. As with human athletes, certain formulations demonstrated increased performance, disease resistance, and better muscle development. Other farms found TMG ineffective, as the specific combination of proteins and other dietary ingredients had a large effect on the role of TMG in muscle gain in animals. The following tables summarize some of the studies showing significant increases in performance measures[77].

One study, adapted from the British Journal of Nutrition (63:339-349, 1990), noted higher ash and protein and less fat in chickens fed the methyl donor TMG than control birds. The higher ash and protein observed in farm animals supplemented with TMG was related to larger skeletal development and muscle mass.

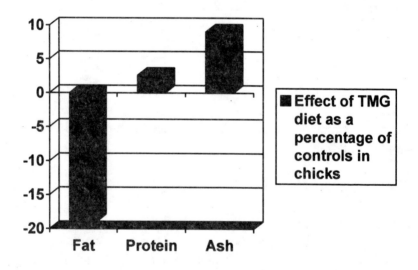

Figure: Effect of TMG on body composition in broiler chickens.

A study with pigs, an animal more similar to people than birds, showed that TMG supplementation could decrease body fat while increasing body protein. Many farms in the U.S. are using TMG in their pig diets so they can produce leaner animals, which the public demands. It may be that TMG can do the same in humans. It is known, however, that improper use of TMG can actually have the exact opposite effect.

The feed industry is a competitive industry, and formulators, farms and nutritionists do not publish everything they know about formulation. Optimizing the effect of methylation (as seen above) by balancing other ingredients in the diet is an art form, and the methods are generally considered proprietary. However, millions of kilograms of TMG are sold per year to the animal feed industry.

Figure: Effect of TMG on body composition in pigs.

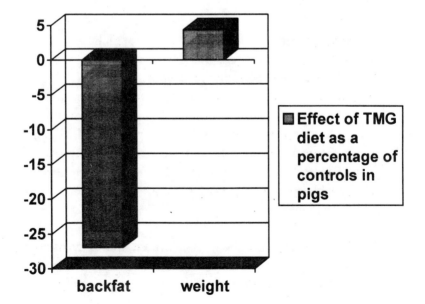

Dietary supplements like TMG can produce a dramatic improvement in muscle gain, result in lower body fat, and increase bone growth.

Report by James Lembeck, D.Ch., C.H.

"On a personal note, I have been using a methyl formula for some time, I weight train four times a week and have found it to be extremely effective in enhancing my ability to perform and recuperate." — Dr. James Lembeck

The goal of every athlete is to increase performance, size and recuperative capacity. These responses can be enhanced by nutritional means, allowing muscles to respond and perform better.

Rigorous training increases the need for a large variety of nutrients, including folate, B-6, B-12, vitamin C, choline and methionine. These nutrients are important partially due to the fact that they supply, or are involved with the production of methyl groups. TMG, a superior methyl donor, is now being used extensively in the feed industry to provide animals methyl donor material to promote and increase muscle growth and protect against osmotic stress (which mimics dehydration). For human athletes, the benefits of TMG go far beyond the possible athletic advantages.

While training, free radicals are formed and extensive tissue damage can occur. This type of stress places a tremendous strain on the methylation process and on other bodily systems, requiring the athlete to eat appropriately and to supply supplemental substances that will protect the tissues from the harm that we "self induce" through training hard. Methyl donors such as TMG could be a major benefit to athletes, assisting in their ability to counteract free radical bombardment and aid in the recuperation process. Recuperation from heavy training requires extensive protein synthesis and repair, a methylation dependent reaction.

In addition, supplementing the diet with TMG helps insure that there are adequate methyl groups for use in the synthesis of several performance enhancing biochemicals. TMG assists in the production of nutritive substances such as acetylcholine, methionine, dimethylglycine, S-adenosylmethionine, carnitine, creatine and phosphatidylcholine. Creatine increases an important energy reservoir in muscle as it enhances the production of ATP (adenosine triphosphate), and carnitine increases the utilization of fatty acids used in the production of energy. Possibly more important than each of these biochemical by-products, however, is the ability of TMG to act as an osmoprotectant (which maintains hydration) to improve performance during intensive training.

High stress workouts can lead to decreased water volume in the cell (dehydration). This is a common problem with high performance athletes. When cellular water content decreases due to any number of factors, intracellular levels of inorganic salts increase. This inhibits enzymatic activity and decreases cellular function at every level. TMG binds to the excess salts inside the cell, creating a more normal environment for physiological processes to occur. It is this salt buffering capacity of TMG that suggested its use for farmed salmon, a fish that must be transplanted during its maturation process from fresh to salt water. Without TMG, a large percentage of salmon die due to the change in water-salt balance inside the cells, whereas the large majority of the TMG fed fish survived the transplantation process.

Cellular regeneration after a hard workout can be accomplished under "optimal conditions" at a fairly rapid rate. This, of course, depends on the age of the individual, their lifestyle, their diet (including supplements), their training regimen and how much rest they get between workouts. In the best of worlds the term "optimal conditions" is as individual as each person who works out. Fortunately, we are living in a period of time that has brought forth tremendous gains in biochemical support through supplementation that offsets the negative effects of our daily routines. TMG is one of the best methyl donors available. It also acts as an osmoprotectant (helps maintain water balance). TMG is a relatively new therapeutic agent in the sports world with wide athletic applications.

APPENDIX IV BALANCING TMG AND METHIONINE

(coccidiosis, the challenge, is a parasitic disease commonly found in the chicken's digestive tract and increases the need for methyl donors).

Balance Between Methyl Donors, TMG, Choline and Methionine is Important[62,63]

Effect of TMG and coccidiosis on concentrations of free methionine and SAM in broiler liver adapted from Virtanen (1997)

Diet	Concentration of methionine or SAM mmole / g wet tissue		
	Methionine	SAM	SAM (challenged)
(1) 0.52% methionine	70	73	118
(2) 0.40% methionine	67	51	97
(3) 0.40% methionine + 0.06% TMG	69	66	100

Disease challenge increased the production of SAM (needed for immune system). Diet (2) did not have enough methyl donors to produce SAM except under challenge. When birds were challenged on Diet (2), they produce sufficient SAM but probably at the expense of other compounds made from homocysteine (such as cysteine, taurine and other sulfur containing material). Diets with the right balance of methionine and TMG such as (3) produce the best bird performance (muscle mass and efficiency) when compared to diets such as (1) when more methyl group are provided from methionine.

Balance is important!

APPENDIX V THE SULFUR GROUP ON HOMOCYSTEINE

CHEMICAL TOXICITY OF HOMOCYSTEINE CHANGED BY ADDING A METHYL (CH₃) GROUP

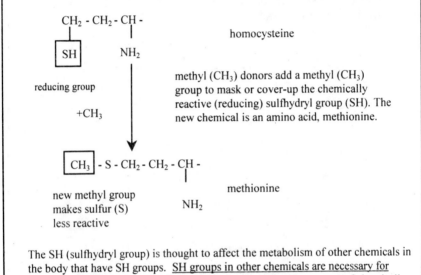

$CH_2 - CH_2 - CH -$

$\boxed{SH}$ NH_2

homocysteine

reducing group

$+CH_3$

methyl (CH_3) donors add a methyl (CH_3) group to mask or cover-up the chemically reactive (reducing) sulfhydryl group (SH). The new chemical is an amino acid, methionine.

$\boxed{CH_3} - S - CH_2 - CH_2 - CH -$

NH_2

methionine

new methyl group makes sulfur (S) less reactive

The SH (sulfhydryl group) is thought to affect the metabolism of other chemicals in the body that have SH groups. <u>SH groups in other chemicals are necessary for proper structure of the walls of blood vessels</u>. Reducing the amount of chemically reactive SH in homocysteine through methylation may partially explain why methylation is so important to reduce the risks of cardiovascular disease.

APPENDIX VI METHYLATION AND DIGESTION

Do You Bloat, Belch or Suffer from Gas?

Betaine and betaine HCl are not the same but they both contain TMG. Betaine HCl contains HCl (hydrochloric acid) which is the same as stomach acid and can be used as a stomach acidifier. However, if you don't need acidification (only a qualified physician could tell you for sure) then it is probably best to avoid betaine HCl. Stomach irritation from betaine HCl has been reported in individuals at the dose required to enhance methylation.

Some middle-aged and older people should be tested to determine if they are producing adequate stomach acid. If you have problems with bloating, belching or gas after a meal and are 50 years of age or older, you may want to let your physician know and specially ask about a stomach acid screen. Many gastrointestinal problems are related to low stomach acidity (pH). Often these problems are treated without considering the need for adjusting stomach acidity.

Betaine HCl is considered an excellent stomach acidifier to aid the digestion of meal in those individuals that have low stomach acidity. Betaine HCl also contains TMG and enhances methylation.

REFERENCES

1.   Graham, I.M., et al. Plasma homocysteine as a risk factor for vascular disease. *Journal of the American Medical Association*, 277(22):1775-1781, 1997.

2.   Miller, A.M., Kelly, G.S. Homocysteine Metabolism: Nutritional modulation and impact on health and disease. *Alternative Medicine Review*, 2(4):234-254, 1997.

3.   Stampfer, M.J. et al. A prospective study of plasma homocyst(e)ine and risk of myocardial infarction in US physicians. *Journal of the American Medical Association*, 268(7):877-81, 1992.

4.   Cooney, C.A. Are somatic cells inherently deficient in methylation metabolism? A proposed mechanism for DNA methylation loss, senescence and aging. *Growth, Development and Aging*, 57(4):261-73, 1993.

5.   Boushey, et al. A quantitative assessment of plasma homocysteine as a risk factor for vascular disease. Probable benefits of increasing folic acid intakes. *Journal of the American Medical Association*, 274(13):1049-1057, 1997.

6.   Finkelstein, J.D., Martin, J.J. Methionine metabolism in mammals. Distribution of homocysteine between competing pathways. *J. Biol. Chem.* 59:9508-9513, 1984.

7.   Finkelstein, J.D., Martin, J.J. Methionine metabolism in mammals. Adaptation to methionine excess. *J. Biol. Chem.* 261:1582-1587, 1986.

8.   Gruber, Edward R. and Raymond, Stephen A. Beyond Cholesterol: Vitamin B6, Arteriosclerosis, and Your Heart. St. Martin's Press: New York, N.Y., 1981.

9.   McCully, K.S. Vascular pathology of homocysteinemia: implications for the pathogenesis of arteriosclerosis. *American Journal of Pathology* 56:111-128, 1969.

10.   McCully, K.S. Homocysteine and vascular disease. *Nature Medicine* 2:386-389, 1996.

11.   Malinow, M.R. Plasma homocyst(e)ine and arterial occlusive diseases: a mini-review. *Clinical Chemistry*, 41(1):173-6, 1995.

12.   Dudman, N.P., et al. Disordered methionine/homocysteine metabolism in premature vascular disease. Its occurrence, cofactor therapy, and enzymology. *Arteriosclerosis and Thrombosis*, 13(9):1253-60, 1993.

13.   van den Berg, M., et al. Combined vitamin B6 plus folic acid therapy in young patients with arteriosclerosis and hyperhomocysteinemia. *Journal of Vascular Surgery*, 20(6):933-40, 1994.

14.   Dudman, N.P.B, et al. Human homocysteine catabolism: Three major pathways and their relevance to development of arterial occlusive disease. *Journal of Nutrition*, 126(4s):1295s-1300s, 1996.

15.   Wilcken, D.E.L, Wilcken, B. The natural history of vascular diasease in homocystinuria and the effects of treatment. *J. Inher. Metab. Dis.* 20:295-300, 1997.

16.   Nygård, O., et al., Plasma homocysteine levels and mortality in patients with coronary artery disease. *N Engl J Med* 337:230-236, 1997.

17.   Duell, P.B., Malinow MR. Homocyst(e)ine: an important risk factor for atherosclerotic vascular disease. *Curr Opin Lipidol* 8(1):28-34, 1997.

18.   Harpel, P.C., et al. Homocysteine and hemostatis: pathogenic mechanisms predisposing to thrombosis. *J Nutr* 126(4s):1285s-1289s, 1996.

19.   Steegers-Theunissen, R.P., et al. Neural tube defects and elevated homocysteine levels in amniotic fluid. *American Journal of Obstetrics and Gynecology*, 172(5):1436-41, 1995.

20.   Mills, J.L. et al. Homocysteine metabolism in pregnancies complicated by neural tube defects. *Lancet*, 345(8943):149-51, January 21, 1995.

21.   Gaby, AR. Preventing and Reversing Osteoporosis. Prima Publishing, 1994.

22.   Brattstrom, L.E. et al. Folic acid responsive postmenopausal homocysteinemia. *Metabolism* 34(11):1073-1077, 1985.

23.   Foster, R.H., Balfour, J.A. Estradiol and dydrogesterone. A review of their combined use as hormone replacement therapy in postmenopausal women. *Drugs Aging*, 11(4):309-332, 1997.

24.   Whiting, S.J, Draper, H.H. Effect of chronic acid load as sulfate or sulfur amino acids on bone metabolism in adult rats. J. Nutr. 111(10):1721-1726, 1981.

25.   Vogel, RI, et al. The effect of folic acid on gingival health. *J. Periodontol*, 47(11):667-668, 1976.

26.   Thomson, M.E., Pack, A.R. Effects of extended systemic and topical folate supplementation on gingivitis of pregnancy. *J. Clin Periodontol* 9(3):275-280, 1982.

27. Pack, A.R. Folate mouthwash: effects on established gingivitis in periodontal patients. J Clin. Periodontol 11(9): 619-628, 1984.

28. Brown, R.S., et al. Nitrendipine-induced gingival hyperplasia. First case report. *Oral Surg Oral Med Oral Pathol* 70(5): 593-596, 1990.

29. Lawrence, D.B., et al. Calcium channel blocker-induced gingival hyperplasia: case report and review of this iatrogenic disease. *J. Fam. Pract*, 39(5):483-488, 1994.

30. Van Poppel, G., Van den Berg, H. Vitamins and cancer. *Cancer letters* 114:195-202, 1997.

31. Mazin, A.L. The loss of all genomic 5-methylcytosine coincides with Hayflick limit of aging cell lines. *Molekulyarnaya Biologiya*, 27(4):895-907, 1993.

32. Mazin, A.L. Genome loses all 5-methlycytosine during life span. How is this related to accumulation of mutations with aging? *Molekulyarnaya Biologiya*, 27(1):160-173, 1993a.

33. Smith, S.S., Baker, D.J. Stalling of human methyltransferase at single-strand conformers from the Huntington's locus. *Biochem Biophys Res Commun*, 234(1):73-78, 1997.

34. Reik, W. et al. Age at onset in Huntington's disease and methylation at D4S95. *J. Med. Genet* 30:185-188, 1993.

35. Farrer, L.A. et al. Inverse relationship between age at onset of Huntington disease and paternal age suggests involvement of genetic imprinting. Am J. Hum Genet. 50(3):528-535, 1992.

36. Chatkupt, S. Parents do matter: genomic imprinting and parental sex effects in neurological disorders. J Neurol. Sci 130(1):1-10, 1995.

37. Stadtman, E.R. Protein oxidation and aging. *Science*, 257: 1120, 1992.

38. Guttering, J.M.C., Halliwell, B., Antioxidants in nutrition, health and disease. Oxford. U.K., 1994

39. Glazer, A.N. Fluoresence-based assay for reactive oxygen species: A protective role for creatinine. *Fed. Am. Soc. Exp. Biol. J.* 2:2487, 1988.

40. Glazer, A.N. Phycoerythrin fluoresence-based assay for reactive oxygen species. In Methiods in Enzymology 186:161. Oxygen Radicals in Biological Systems. Academic Press. San Diego,CA. 1990.

41. Miller, J.K., Brezezinska-Slebodzinska, E., Madsen, F.C. Oxidative stress, antioxidants and animal function. *J. Dairy Sci.* 76:2812, 1993.

42. Wayner, D.D.M., Burton, G.W. et al. The relative contributions of vitamin E, urate, ascorbate and proteins to the total peroxyl radical trapping antioxidant activity of human blood plasma. *Biochem. Biophys. Acta* 934:408, 1987.

43. Taylor, A., Lipman, R.D., et al. Dietary calorie restriction in the emory mouse: effects of lifespan, eye lens cataract prevalence and progression, levels of ascorbate, glutathioine, glucose, and glycohemoglobin, tail collagen breaktime, DNA and RNA oxidation, skin integrity, fecundity and cancer. *Mechanisms of Aging and Development* 79:33-57

44. Miller, J.K., Madsen, F.C. Transition metals, oxidative status and animal health: Do alterations in plasma fast-acting antioxidants lead to disease in livestock?, Biotechnology in the Feed Industry, Proc. Alltech's 10th Ann. Symp., Eds. Lyons, T.P., Jacques, K.A. Nottingham University Press, UK (page 283).

45. Weitzman, S.A., et al. Free radical adducts induce alterations in DNA cytosine methylation. *Proc. Natl. Acad. Sci.* USA 91:1261-1264, 1994.

46. Romanenko, E.B., et al. Effect of sphingomyelin and antioxidants on the in vitro and in vivo DNA methylation. Biochemistry and Molecular Biology Int'l. 35(1):87-94, 1995.

47. Kagan, B.L, et al. Oral S-adenosylmethionine in depression: a randomized double-blind, placebo-controlled trial. *American Journal of Psychiatry*, 147(5):591-5, 1990.

48. Brandes, L.J. et al. Stimulation of malignant growth in rodents by antidepressant drugs at clinically relevant doses. *Cancer Research*, 52(13):796-800, 1992.

49. Kishi, T., et al. Effect of betaine on S-adenosylmethionine levels in the cerebrospinal fluid in a patient with methylenetetrahydrofolate reductase deficiency and peripheral neuropathy. *Journal of Inherited Metabolic Disease*, 17(5): 560-5, 1994

50. , Barak, A.J. et al. Dietary betaine promotes generation of hepatic S-adenosylmethionine and protects the liver from ethanol-induced fatty infiltration. *Alcoholism, Clinical and Experimental Research*, 17(3):552-5,1993.

51. Barak, A.J. et al. Betaine, ethanol, and the liver: A review. *Alcohol.* 13(4):395-398, 1996.

52. Wallnoefer, H. Hanusch M. Essential phospholips in the treatment of hepatic disease. *Med Monatsschrift* 27(3), 131-6, 1973.

53. Kidd, P.M. Phosphatidylcholine (PC), versatile cel membrane nutrient: Its benefits for the liver. Report published by Lucas Meyer, 1996.

54. Wise, CK, Cooney, C., et al. Measuring S-adenosylmethionine in whole blood, red blood cells and cultured cells using a fast preparation method and high performance liquid chromatography. *Journal of Chromatography* B 696:145-152, 1997.

55. Roubenoff, R. et al. Abnormal vitamin B6 status in rheumatoid cachexia. *Arthritis and Rheumatism*, 38:105-109, 1995.

56. Brijlal, S. et al. Flavin metabolism during respiratory infection in mice. *British J. Nutrition*, 76:453-462, 1996.

57. Klasing, K.C. Nutritional aspects of leukocytic cytokines. *J. Nutrition*, 118:1436-1446, 1988.

58. Cooney, C. Personal communication, 1997.

59. Feenstra, A. et al. In vitro methylation inhibits the promotor activity of a cloned intracisternal A-particle LTR. *Nucleic Acids Research*, 14:4343-4352, 1986.

60. Mays-Hoopes, et al. Methylation and rearrangement of mouse intracisternal a particle genes in development, aging and myeloma. *Molecular and Cellular Biiology*, 3:1371-1380, 1983.

61. Hadchouel, M., et al. Material inhibition of hepatitis B surface antigen gene expression in transgenic mice correlates with de novo methylation. *Nature*, 329:454-456, 1987.

62. Vertanen, E. Continuing the debate: betaine, methionine and choline. *Feed Milling International*, March, pg 14-16, 1997.

63. Virtanen, e., et al. The effect of betaine and salinomycin during coccidiosis in broilers. Poultry Science 75(suppl 1):149 (abs), 1996.

64. Davenport, R. Personal Communication, 1998.

65. Ubbink, J.B. The role of vitamins in the pathogenesis and treatment of hyperhomocyst(e)inaemia. *J. Inher. Metab. Dis* 20:316-325, 1997.

66. Doscherholmen A., Hagen, P.S. A dual mechanism of vitamin B12 plasma absorption. *J. Clin. Invest.* 36:1551-1557, 1957.

67. Bostom, A.G. et al. Post-methionine load hyperhomocysteinemia in persons with normal fasting total homocysteine: initial results from the NHLBI family heart study. *Atherosclerosis*, 116:147-151, 1995.

68. Henderson, L.M. Vitamin B6. In: Present knowledge in Nutrition, 5th Ed.,pages 303-317, The Nutrition Foundation, Inc. Washington, D.C.

69.   Leklem, J.E. Vitamin B6: Reservoirs, receptors, and red-cell reactions. *Ann. NY Acad. Sci*, 669:34-43, 1992.

70.   Haigney, M., et al. Tissue magnesium levels and the arrhythmic substrate in humans. *Journal of Cardiovascular Electrophysiology*, 8(9):980-986, 1997.

71.   Lieu, P.L. et al. Phospholipids, phospholipid methylation and taurine content in synaptosomes of developing rat brain. In: Taurine. Editors: Lombardini, J.B., et al. Plenum Press, New York,1992.

72.   Schwade, Steve. *Prevention*, p.74, July 1994.

73.   Alfthan, G., et al. Plasma Homocysteine and cardiovascular disease mortality. *Lancet* 349:397, 1997.

74.   Nygård, O., et al. Total plasma homocysteine and cardiovascular risk profile. The Hordaland homocysteine study. *JAMA* 274(19):1526-33,1995.

75.   Perry, I.J., et al. Prospective study of serum total homocysteine concentration and risk of stroke in middle-aged British men. *Lancet* 346:1395-98, 1997

76.   Vaccaro, O. et al. Moderate hyperhomocysteinaemia and retinopathy in insulin-dependent diabetes. *Lancet* 349:1102-1103, 1997.

77.   The Betafin Briefing. Finnsugar Bioproducts, 1996.

78.   Kim, M-J, et al. Adult-onset energy restriction of rhesus monkey alternates oxidative stress-induced cytokine expression by perhipheral blood mononuclear cells. *J. Nutrition* 127:2293-2301, 1997.

79.   Matthews, J.O., et al. Interactive effects of betaine and monensin in uninfected and Eimeria acervulina-infected chicks. *Poultry Science* 76:1014-1019, 1997.

80.   Wiklud, O. et al. N-acetylcysteine treatment lowers plasma homocysteine but not serum lipoprotein(a) levels. *Atherosclerosis*, 119:99-106, 1996.

81.   Jakubowski, H. Metabolism of homocysteine thiolactone in human cell cultures. Possible mechanism for pathological consequences of elevated homocysteine levels *J. Bio. Chem.* 272:1935-1942, 1997.

OTHER REFERENCES

Baylin, S.B. et al. Abnormal patterns of DNA methylation in human neoplasia: potential consequence for tumor progression. *Cancer Cells* 383-390, 1991.

Boers, G.H. Hyperhomocysteinaemia: a newly recognized risk factor for vascular disease. *Netherlands Journal of Medicine*, 45(1):34-41, 1994.

Bottiglieri, T. et al. The clinical potential of ademetionine (S-adenosylmethionine) in neurological disorders. *Drugs*, 48(2):137-52, 1994.

Butterworth, C.E. Jr. Folate status, women's health, pregnancy outcome, and cancer. *Journal of the American College of Nutrition*, 12(4):438-41, 1993.

Eskes, T.K. Possible basis for primary prevention of birth defects with folic acid. Mills *Fetal Diagnosis and Therapy*, 9(3):149-54, 1994.

Franken, D.G. et al. Treatment of mild hyperhomocysteinemia in vascular disease patients. *Arteriosclerosis and Thrombosis*, 14(3):465-70, 1994.

Friedel, Heather et al. S-Adenosyl-L-Methionine: A review of its pharmacological properties and therapeutic potential in liver dysfunction and affective disorders in relation to its physiological role in cell metabolism. *Drugs*, 38(3):389-416, 1989.

Giovannucci, Edward et al. Folate, Methionine and Alcohol Intake and Risk of Colorectal Adenoma. *Journal of the National Cancer Institute*, 85(11):875-84, 1993.

Holme, E. et al. Betaine for treatment of homocystinuria caused by methylenetetrahydrofolate reductase deficiency. *Archives of Disease in Childhood*, 64:1061-4, 1989.

Lucock, M.D. et al. The methylfolate axis in neural tube defects: in vitro characterisation and clinical investigation. *Biochemical Medicine and Metabolic Biology*, 52(2):101-14, 1994.

Montero, Brens C. et al. Homocystinuria: effectiveness of the treatment with pyridoxine, folic acid, and betaine. *Anales Espanoles de Pediatria*, 39(1):37-41, 1993.

Reynolds, E. H. and Stramentinoli, G. Folic acid, S-adenosylmethionine and affective disorder. *Psychological Medicine*, 13:705-710, 1983.

Reed, S.M., Glick, J.N. Fluoxetine and reactivation of the herpes simplex virus. Am. J. Psychiatry 49:949-950, 1991.

Scott, J.M. et al. Folic acid metabolism and mechanisms of neural tube defects. CIBA Foundation Symposium, 181:180-91, 1994.

Steegers-Theunissen, R.P. et al. Maternal hyperhomocysteinemia: a risk factor for neural-tube defects? *Metabolism: Clinical and Experimental*, 43(12):1475-80, 1994.

Ueland, P.M. and Refsum. H. Plasma Homocysteine, a risk factor for vascular disease: plasma levels in health, disease, and drug therapy. *Journal of Laboratory and Clinical Medicine*, 144(5);473-501, 1989.

INDEX

RESOURCES

Please look for future publications from The Research Corner.

Interesting Web sites:

The Research Corner
www.pacificnet.net/~trc

The National Health Federation and the Database of Miracles
www.healthfreedom.org